FANON

FANON

**Peter
Geismar**

GROVE PRESS, INC.,
NEW YORK

Grateful acknowledgment is made to the following for permission to reprint copyrighted material:

Grove Press, Inc. for *The Wretched of the Earth* by Frantz Fanon. Translations from the French by Constance Farrington. Copyright © 1963 by Présence Africaine.

Monthly Review Press for *Toward the African Revolution* by Frantz Fanon. English translation copyright © 1967 by Monthly Review Press. Copyright © 1964 by François Maspero.

New Directions Publishing Corporation for *Journey to the End of Night* by Louis-Ferdinand Céline. Translated by J. H. P. Marks. Copyright 1934, © 1961 by Louis-Ferdinand Céline.

This edition is published by arrangement with The Dial Press.

ISBN: 0-394-17396-1
Library of Congress Catalog Card Number: 70-144373
First Evergreen Black Cat Edition 1971
Second Printing
Manufactured in the United States of America
Distributed by Random House, Inc., New York

This biography is drawn largely from interviews and conversations. There are many whom I would like to thank for their patience with questions, and their helpfulness. But the essence of Fanon remains controversy, so that it would be unfair to link individual names with the subjective conclusions of the work. Still, I will mention my editors, especially Lois Silverman, whose criticisms prevented me from publishing an encyclopedia of all that was not relevant to Fanon.

The greatness of a man is to be found not in his acts but in his style. Existence does not resemble a steadily rising curve, but a slow, and sometimes sad, series of ups and downs.

I have a horror of weaknesses—I understand them, but I do not like them.

I do not agree with those who think it possible to live life at an easy pace. I don't want this. . . .

—FRANTZ FANON
1952

Contents

FANON

Introduction

In a hectic, violent, and very short lifetime, Frantz Fanon wrote four books that serve as an essential record of the psychological and material costs of colonization, as a study of the dynamics of rapid social change, and as an outline for a different future for the colonial areas.

Fanon's writings were first fully appreciated within the Western civilization that he attacked so violently: His books have become required reading for the black revolutionaries in the United States who consider their people as part of the Third World—the term commonly used today to designate the whole of the underdeveloped world. The American blacks do live in ghetto colonies in the heart of the mother country; they are exploited by foreign white businesses and ruled by foreign white politicians and police forces—foreign certainly to Harlem, Watts, or Bedford-Stuyvesant. The black Left in America is very much aware of the crucial theme in Fanon's later works—that political independence for the colonized must be the precursor to economic and social revolution in the underdeveloped areas. Though commonly thought of as anarchistic or nihilistic, the Black Panther party is a tightly disciplined, nonracist movement with a socialist ideology. Huey Newton, one of the jailed leaders, said that

> there is no hope for cultural or individual expression, or even hope that the black people can exist as a unique entity, as long as bureaucratic capitalism is in control.*

All of the Panther leaders, according to Ronald Steel,

> have been deeply influenced by the black psychiatrist from Martinique who died in the service of the Algerian revolution. *The Wretched of the Earth* is a kind of revolutionary bible. . . .†

Fanon's later writings dealing with the future of the Third World contrast sharply with his first book, *Black Skin, White Masks*, published in 1952, which is actually the diary of a black intellectual recovering from the trauma of a delayed introduction to the white Western world. His second book, *A Dying Colonialism*, is an extended commentary on a society undergoing a thorough restructuring, an original description of a colonial people winning self-determi-

* *The Movement* (August, 1968).
† *The New York Review of Books* (September 11, 1969).

nation. The author's troubled conscience on racial matters has dissolved in a furious movement toward revolution. By the time of *The Wretched of the Earth,* Fanon is convinced that the Third World's agricultural masses have replaced the urban proletariat as the dynamic force in modern history. An elaboration of this theory is available in *Toward the African Revolution,* a collection of Fanon's articles showing his development of thought from the time of his departure from French bourgeois society to his death in 1961.

Joby Fanon, speaking in very precise tones from behind his large desk in the Customs Division of the Ministry of Finance in Paris, warned me against exaggerating the unusual qualities of his younger brother: "You know," he said, "Frantz was not a superman." Joby Fanon then went on to relate incident after incident which to me contradicted this opening statement. Frantz Fanon was very attractive and an extremely good athlete. Women were drawn to him in unusual numbers. He was without fear for his own life. Wounded twice in the Second World War, he was decorated for "Brilliant Conduct" in the last months of the fighting. He wrote three plays; became a medical doctor; then a psychiatrist. Before he was thirty-seven he had four major books and numerous articles to his credit. He had made more than fifteen contributions in original research to psychiatric journals and conferences. He worked seventeen hours a day, had an astounding memory, a cutting sense of humor, an unusual stage presence.

Fanon was strongly influenced by Nietzsche. In *Thus Spake Zarathustra* he saw the superman as one who is not crippled by an excess of reasons for *not* acting. One who still knows passion, but is able to control it. One who stands above the masses by his ability to throw off the shackles of conventional morality and religion. One who has ideas and the will to carry them out. Fanon, too, was of Sartre's and Camus' generation, which considered theory secondary to action. Fanon himself said that theory grew out of actions and that actions had to be evaluated in terms of their reconstructing a consciousness of the human condition. All of Fanon's most original ideas were the result of his own life. The essence of his writing becomes clearer as one learns of the different stages of his existence.

I

Martinique

At first it could be a small city on the French Riviera: high rocky slopes spotted with green vegetation descending steeply into a very light blue sea. But as a ship enters the harbor, the resemblance melts away: The trees at the base of the hills are thicker, more tropical, the hills covered with shanties. There are few substantial dwellings beyond the harbor area itself. One part of the bay is reserved for a small number of large and elegant private yachts, and that can be the last impression of Europe before disembarking into a different world. The Martinican sun is hot and bright; the port crowded with black workers balancing huge weights on their heads and struggling toward waiting trucks. Strange sounds assail the ears: the Creole patois, a mixture of Spanish, French, and English that developed as the common language of the African slaves brought to the Caribbean after the seventeenth century. An American or European hears many words he understands, but loses the meaning of the phrase. For Creole is spoken quickly, with a harsh, gutteral accent—at least to the Western way of thinking. And that was Fanon's point: We use language as another means of dominating colonial areas. It has always been made clear in Europe and the colonies that the native can not rule himself because he does not speak a civilized tongue. The Caribbean black is only considered part of the human species as he becomes fluent in a purer form of French, English, or Spanish. In Martinique (as in Guadeloupe and Guiana, the other overseas departments of France), language is closely associated with class structure. The poorer islanders speak the patois; the assimilated bourgeoisie use French except when giving orders to inferiors. European values are continually emphasized within the Third World as being the only true values. Disembarking at Fort-de-France, the capital of Martinique, a person having good French or English is whisked through customs, while Creole-speaking blacks are searched for contraband goods. The customs people are extremely polite and speak the clearest French imaginable—to visitors at least.

Beyond the customs headquarters there are numerous open-fronted shanties, the workers' bars, between the warehouses of Fort-de-France's port. The only thing served there is the one-hundred-proof rum made on the island which goes for about a nickel a glass. By ten in the morning the bars are packed and each one seems to be decorated with one or two of the clientele, passed out in the corners. The more "serious" workers only have a glass at a time and can return to their monotonous duties of unloading ships. A visitor makes his way out of this desolate scene, skirting the twenty-foot-high, moss-covered walls of the fort that protected French interests on the island for three hundred years, to the center of the city, the Savanne, a vast dusty square lined with worm-eaten tamarinds, one end marked by the inevitable French war memorial statue. The Savanne is bordered by the more substantial structures of Fort-de-France—four- and five-story whitewashed banks, shipping companies, and other offices separated by a few hotels and numerous cafés. Everything seems slightly dilapidated though; even the statue is not quite erect. It is a parody of a French provincial city with architecture not quite up to the standards of the Second Empire. In the play, *No Exit,* Sartre used the decor of a Second-Empire-style living room to depict Hell.

Leaving the Savanne, where Fanon spent some part of his youth lounging and talking with other students, the visitor passes into the older section of town with its narrow streets and two-foot-deep open gutters filled by swiftly running dirty water. At midday the city's open-air market is going at full blast with as many as fifty merchants, mostly women, selling all kinds of fruits and vegetables piled in front of them on the ground or stacked in little carts. The more prosperous vendors are protected from the fierce sun by umbrellas; the less successful are trying to dispose of tiny bits of sugar cane or half-rotted fruit that they salvaged from the end of yesterday's market. Everywhere one can see large sores on the peoples' legs, the ostentatious marks of malnutrition. On one side of the market square, next to a canal that runs through the city, sea food is sold to some of the wealthier islanders.

In little streets off the market place there are a few butcher shops with mostly white clientele; the average islander cannot afford meat.

The butchers' customers are the *békès*, the nineteenth-century, wealthy, white aristocracy that owns three quarters of the island's productive land, the larger stores, the construction companies, the newspaper, and most of the port facilities. The *békès*, an ingrown, unfriendly group, hostile even to the upper class of the metropolitan territory, have their own private bar on the Savanne above the city's best restaurant. They descend to dine but return above to socialize. Out of a total island population of 300,000, there are about 1,000 rich *békès*, and perhaps 25,000 other people, mostly black, who could be classified as middle class. The small property owners and civil servants, such as the Fanon family, are usually highly patriotic French citizens. But they are hard pressed financially since all the manufactured goods and many of the groceries (all the meat) are imported from France, where the prices were high to begin with. Fanon, when he first began to think about such things, wondered why the middle class did not resent metropolitan France's relationship with the island. It was simply because the bourgeoisie had been taught to care, most of all, about its relative position in Martinique—far above the masses. French rule was necessary to preserve the privileges, large and small, of both the black and white upper classes.

Fanon rarely discussed issues like these with his mother, a mild-mannered, heavy-set woman who likes to smile. Today, she lives in a small, neat house just outside of the city, and she is a strange mixture of emotions: happy with the conventional careers of her six living children; proudest of Frantz Fanon, the author and psychiatrist. Mme. Fanon considers herself just another French citizen living a normal life in a provincial city. Her family has been much more successful than those that surround her. She was happiest, no doubt, when Frantz was practicing medicine in Martinique; but she would defend him, quietly, after he turned against the French. When I visited her in 1969, she first showed me her son's decorations from the French army in the Second World War; then a copy of *The Wretched of the Earth,* a scathing attack on all that France stands for. The island knows about the author of this book and hates him. The Fort-de-France Public Library only has Fanon's first book; the stores there will not carry any of his publications; nor will they order such material for a customer. I was forced to move from my hotel on the Savanne after the *patron* found out the nature of my research. But Mme. Fanon exhibits no scars from social isolation; her strength and self-confidence are impressive. She appears to share Frantz Fanon's courage if not his convictions. At any rate, it is his photograph that dominates her living room.

The portrait—a three-quarter-length view—was taken in 1952, when he was twenty-seven years old. Fanon has on a grayish suit; he is thin, has a pale complexion and dark deep-set eyes. He already has a slightly receding, curly hairline. He looks extremely proper and shy, in stark contrast with a later photograph used by Grove Press on the dust jacket of *The Wretched of the Earth.* This second photo is of a furious Fanon with growling, heavy lips; a deep, furrowed forehead; flashing, hostile eyes; and a vicious-looking slash mark on the left cheek. In Algeria I asked one of Fanon's closest friends to give me a description of the man. He seemed perplexed, answering, "It's hard. His face was always changing, especially when he talked. You know, as he told stories he'd act out the parts of the people he was describing. He could be like Marcel

Marceau." Not satisfied, I showed the friend the Grove Press photograph: "Is that Fanon?"

"No, no . . . that was his idea of what a black militant should look like." The friend was embarrassed at what had slipped out of his mouth, and he had to reiterate the whole explanation about Fanon's mobile features, acting abilities. . . .

Joby Fanon is also built like an athlete, but broader in the chest and stronger than his younger brother Frantz. He has more delicate features and a touch of graying hair above his temples. He has worked for the French Ministry of Finance's Customs Division in a number of different capacities in several countries. Always well-dressed and articulate, Joby at first seems cynical about radical politics and black nationalism. But the sarcasm hides a profound anger over the condition of the one thing that he cares for most—his homeland, Martinique. Joby Fanon has many of the characteristics attributed to his dead brother. When he begins to talk, it is as if he had inhaled a huge amount of air; the listener feels the impact of each syllable ejaculated from deep within. He is a charismatic speaker with a range of knowledge from his own field of market economics, through the history of black poetry in several languages, to the specifics of political documents such as the Evian Accords, which ended the French-Algerian war in 1962.

In 1952, shortly after defending the thesis that is required of all medical students before they become doctors in France, Frantz Fanon took the four-hour train ride from Lyons to Paris to meet with Joby so they could return to Martinique for the Carnival, and a rest. Frantz presented Joby with a copy of his medical thesis and also brought one home to Félix, his other older brother, who is taller, with Arabic facial features, and less voluble. Félix completed a technical education in the island's school system, then entered the civil service there as an engineer for the Department of Public Works. On the cover of the seventy-five-page thesis, Frantz wrote,

> To my brother Félix,
> I offer this work—
> The greatness of a man is to be found not in his acts but in his style. Existence does not resemble a steadily rising curve, but a slow, and sometimes sad, series of ups and downs.
> I have a horror of weaknesses—I understand them, but I do not like them.
> I do not agree with those who think it possible to live life at an easy pace. I don't want this. I don't think you do either. . . .

The beginning of this dedication is startling—especially since it is found on the cover of the most boring piece of writing Fanon ever produced, a conventional survey of certain physical nervous disorders. Fanon did hate weaknesses, physical and spiritual, and was usually successful in avoiding them.

There are also three Fanon sisters, married and integrated into Martinican middle-class existence, as well as another younger brother, Willy, working for the Ministry of Education in Paris. It is an assimilated and conventional family—to outward appearances at least. In conversations, however, the brothers tend to agree with Frantz's analyses of European racism; are uncomfortable with French rule in Martinique. Joby Fanon has worked with a separatist movement on the island; after 1967 he was forbidden, by administrative decree, to return to his homeland. A prisoner in the French Ministry of Finance! (He cannot be fired from this job for two reasons: he passed one of the highest civil service examinations given in France; and there is no one to replace him in the tremendously intricate task of assessing the true value of corporations wishing to establish themselves in France or the Common Market.) One has the feeling that Joby Fanon would not be unhappy in a revolutionary situation. It appears too that certain of the offspring of the Fanon brothers will look to their well-known uncle as a model for their own future development. In the United States the black revolutionaries, Malcolm X and others, come from the streets and the prisons; Europe has an older tradition of producing the same kind of leadership from within the second and third generations of the educated bourgeoisie.

In Martinican society Fanon's family could best be described as upper middle class. When he was still in school there, they had a spacious apartment in the center of the city with a cook and a woman who came to clean. His father's salary as a government *fonctionnaire* was not high; but his mother, working as a shopkeeper, provided the family with the extra income for such luxuries as meat on weekends, and the movies three times a year. The island's primary education was free, but the Fanon children were part of the 4 per cent of the young population able to pay the small tuition for the *lycée*. To be sure, it was a black *lycée* with the *békès* children carefully segregated in another private religious school.

The Fanon brothers' earlier education and social life were carefully supervised by parents and teachers. Frantz's and Joby's one claim to freedom was that they usually managed to skip out of religious education on Thursdays. Still there was not much freedom to think in this period: the only books available were the official school texts concentrating on metropolitan history and literature. The public library had a small collection of fiction, but the churchlike atmosphere there repelled younger readers. There could be little profound dissatisfaction with this comfortable island existence until distance provided a different perspective. . . .

Frantz and Joby Fanon were short on cash from the expensive voyage back to Martinique in 1952. Frantz became restless too. He rented an office in Vauclin in the southern part of the island where his mother's family had come from, and took patients as a general practitioner. He continued to read and study in psychiatry. Fanon was being trained within a school that worked toward synthesizing Freud and Marx: The disturbed individual had to be rehabilitated within his proper social context. Believing that neuroses could be related to ever-present environmental circumstances more than to youthful trauma, Fanon wrote:

> The neurotic structure of an individual is simply the elaboration, the formation, the eruption within the ego of conflictual clusters arising in part out of the environment and in part out of the purely personal way in which the individual reacts to these influences.*

Strongly influenced by Jung, he wanted to reform the theories of the collective unconscious too. Whereas Jung located this unconscious in the inherited cerebral matter, Fanon called it the "sum of prejudices, myths, collective attitudes of a given group." He believed that

> The Jews who have settled in Israel will produce in less than a hundred years a collective unconscious

* _Black Skin, White Masks_ (New York: Grove Press, 1967), p. 81.

different from the ones they had before 1945 in the countries which they were forced to leave.*

Attitudes and fears made up the unconscious; and these could change with a reformed society. Given a certain amount of time, scars in personalities could heal and the health of the unconscious improve. For Fanon, the collective unconscious was a social and cultural phenomenon; not inherited, but acquired. The Martinicans, both black and white, had what he termed a "European" collective unconscious; one that suspected darkness of being evil and associated blackness with sin, an unconscious that made the black man into a sexual animal rather than a rational human being. The Martinican black was forever in combat with his own image, his acquired sense of moral degeneration.

Fanon linked Jung's theories with Adler's assumption that all neuroses involve some sort of final goal for which the neurotic must unsuccessfully strive. In the Antilles, the chain of Caribbean islands including Martinique and Guadeloupe, the final goal was whiteness. The Negro could not exist in himself but only in his attempt to become white—to speak like whites, act like whites, dress like whites, live like the whites. He would even compare himself with his fellow against the pattern of the white man. All of this continually re-enforced a collective inferiority complex.

Black Skin, White Masks is Fanon reasoning that there is something desperately wrong with French society as reflected in its administration of the overseas department of Martinique. The book developed out of a series of separate essays and speeches after 1948; Fanon edited them into a unified work in 1951. While a university student at

Ibid., p. 188.

Lyons he had come to understand the perverted nature of his earlier education in Fort-de-France. Since the nineteenth century the French have sought to assimilate chosen individuals from the colonies by reassuring them that, despite their primitive heritages, they could become Frenchmen with all the glorious advantages of a Western existence. Assimilation is made to sound egalitarian and revolutionary; in practice, it is a method of controlling the colonial masses while Europeans exploit the labor and resources of their lands.

As a young child learning to read and write, the one phrase that recurred in Fanon's school work was "Je suis Français." These were the first three words he learned to spell; the first three words he could read. He and his friends, some of whose fathers worked in the Martinican sugar fields, sat in classrooms decorated with pictures of the wine harvest in Bordeaux and winter sports in Grenoble. They were taught the history of France as though it were their own history. At home Fanon and his brothers and sisters learned French songs. Sometimes if they misbehaved they were warned not "to act like niggers." When the nineteen-year-old Fanon left the Antilles in 1944, he still hoped he was an ordinary (white) French citizen.

A few years later, though aware of the misleading nature of the early education, the effects of it were strong enough so that he still wished to be French:

> What is all this talk of a black people, of a Negro nationality? I am a Frenchman. I am interested in French culture, French civilization, the French people. . . . I am personally interested in the future of France, in French values, in the French nation.*

Ibid., p. 203.

In 1952, as he re-examined life in Martinique, Fanon had
some second thoughts about this paragraph he had composed earlier in Lyons. The metropolitan territory had
little to offer his brothers; there was not a sign of industrialization on the island. The sugar that he used in his
morning's coffee had traveled to Marseilles or Lille for
refining and back to the Antilles for consumption. Half
the male population there was unemployed. Those with
jobs could count on no more than a hundred dollars a
month for a seven-day work week and a fourteen-hour
work day. There was full employment for only two months
in the year, during the sugar harvest. The rest of the time
many Martinicans lived on credit. In the harvest period
merchants automatically seized the salaries of those who
had borrowed. A hundred years ago slavery was outlawed
in the French colonies; in the Antilles a much more efficient wage slavery replaced the older kind of servitude.

Since there are always small pieces of sugar cane or
rotted fruit to be found in the countryside, no one dies of
starvation there, but the masses of agricultural workers
and many city dwellers are undernourished. Their diet
has very little protein content; three fourths of the whole
Martinican population get less than 1,800 calories a day;
they are hungry.

> The Martinican is a Frenchman [Fanon wrote while
> at Lyons], he wants to remain part of the French un-
> ion; he asks only one thing, he wants the idiots and
> exploiters to give him a chance to live like a human
> being.*

The return to Fort-de-France and Vauclin convinced Fanon of a very simple political truth: that exploiters don't

Ibid., p. 202.

agreeably give up exploitation. This, and its more subtle implications, became a major scheme in all his later writings, so different from *Black Skin, White Masks.*

The first book is a poetical and philosophical tract with an emphasis on psychology rather than politics. Fanon was still in the shadow of the most distinguished teacher from the Lycée of Fort-de-France, the writer Aimé Césaire. The respect for the professor was harmful only when Fanon tried to imitate his style: Some of the weakest passages of *Black Skin, White Masks* are modeled on the alternating prose and poetry of Césaire's autobiography, a way of writing that Fanon never perfected. In this first book, Fanon becomes so entranced with the sound of words that he sometimes obscures all content:

> No, from the point of view adopted here, there is no black problem. Or at any rate if there is one it concerns the whites only accidentally. It is a story that takes place in darkness, and the sun that is carried within me must shine into the smallest crannies.*

The rest of the book is about the black problem that has been created by the whites. One could excuse this play on words were it not for more severe impositions.

> The explosion will not happen today [Fanon writes in the introduction]. It is too soon . . . or too late.
> I do not come with timeless truths.
> My consciousness is not illuminated with ultimate radiances.
> Nevertheless, in complete composure, I think it would be good if certain things were said.
> These things I am going to say, not shout. For it is a long time since shouting has gone out of my life.
> So very long. . . .†

Ibid., p. 29.
†*Ibid.,* p. 7.

It is calm, resigned, aesthetic writing, but not Fanon's own. The author, only twenty-seven, was not at all composed. Frantz Fanon's mind always raced ahead; his writing could hardly keep up; in fact, few people can decipher the desperate wriggling of his letters. Sometimes when he spoke he would have to stop, totally exhausted at what had suddenly poured out of him. Even his short notes contained many unrelated ideas flowing through his mind at the same time. He had many things to shout about. His name is important today because he did shout, and with much more power than in these early passages. The introduction to *Black Skin, White Masks* might have been a sudden attack of hyper-romanticism. But when Francis Jeanson, one of Fanon's first editors, asked him to clarify a phrase in the body of the book, Fanon answered,

> I cannot explain that phrase more fully. I try, when I write such things, to touch the nerves of my reader. . . . That's to say irrationally, almost sensually.*

For another explanation of the obscurity of this early writing, return to Fanon's own comments on the use of language in the colonial context. He made it clear that the native's virility, power, intellectual prestige, and social standing were dependent on his knowledge and facility with European tongues. Aimé Césaire, in this respect, was the black king of Martinique; his mastery of French surpassed that of most of the contemporary writers in the metropolitan territory. Fanon tried to emulate Césaire. Consciously too: The first book begins with a quotation

---

*Quoted in Jeanson's preface to the French edition of *Black Skin, White Masks* (Paris, Editions du Seuil, 1952).

from Césaire's *Discours sur le colonialisme;* in the next two hundred pages there are close to twenty citations from the master's works. At one point Fanon constructs a dialogue between his manuscript and another of Césaire's works. There was no rivalry: Fanon only wanted to be like Césaire. But the younger Martinican's writing is vastly improved when he moves away from the professor.

It was easier for Fanon to establish his own political personality independent from Césaire's. Although closely allied as two of the few intellectuals who had returned to the island and cared about its future, they chose different paths toward the same political goals. Césaire was part of what we would call the Old Left, Fanon of the New Left. Césaire became mayor of Fort-de-France and a deputy of the French parliament as a candidate of the Communist Party. Fanon became a communist through joining a revolution—one that was miles apart from the French Communists' strictures on political upheaval. Fanon's political theory developed out of his life after 1954; his first allegiances were to the agricultural masses of the Third World. He had learned a lot from Césaire, though, and was always in awe of the black poet's demagogic and artistic abilities. Césaire, for his part, broke with the C.P. in 1956 because of its disregard for the Third World. Neither Fanon nor Césaire was politically inflexible; they agreed on the kind of better society that they were working for; they shared the same enemies.

In Martinique, Fanon assessed the strength of the enemy as being much greater than did Césaire. Besides the French army and the police force, the *békès* could rely on more subtle weapons for keeping control of the island. The indoctrination of the primary education was continued by the mass media, the state-controlled radio as well as the privately owned newspaper. The masses were continually appeased by the liberal distribution of the territory's one important manufactured product, 100-proof rum. In Fanon's time, a quart of this potent drug could be purchased for less than forty cents. The more distressing life became for a Martinican, the deeper he lowered himself into alcoholism. Those without the money for another bottle of rum would settle for free drinks from friends. Island society enforced this kind of generosity. The Martinicans with regular employment preferred to drink in groups in cafés or bars, most of which were open all night to accommodate customers who passed out. One mixed straight rum with a little sugar syrup to make the standard drink called "punch." Only the bourgeoisie could afford to weaken this concoction with ice, which was more expensive than the rum.

There were obvious difficulties in attempting to politicize a mass of people under these conditions. The example of Aimé Césaire, who remained the highest elected official in Martinique for almost two decades without affecting substantial reform on the island, was proof. The workers voted for him simply because they knew he was famous in France as well as Martinique. The masses supported him despite the fact that he was a Communist, or traitor, as the *békès* termed him. Césaire linked Martinique's future to that of the working class in France; as a Marxist, he believed that the revolution would have to occur in the industrialized metropolitan territory first: The benefits would then flow outward to the Third World. In 1956, when Césaire finally broke with the C.P., he formed the Progressive Party dedicated first to Caribbean socialism. The Martinicans seemed to go along with him, not caring much about the name of his party. He had become his own peculiar institution on the island, always touring the constituency under the blazing sun with his familiar heavy dark suit and dark tie. Eternally optimistic about the future; eternally arousing the savage ire of those to whom he posed no real threat.

Later in his life, when he was attempting to promote Third World unity above nationalism in order to combat Western neocolonialism, Fanon was accused of lacking a sense of *Realpolitik*. Sometimes there were grounds for the accusation. But his judgments and actions in Martinique showed that Fanon could sense the necessity of strategic retreat, a most important quality of effective politics. From conversations with patients, from discussions with Césaire, from the local newspaper and radio, Fanon was increasingly convinced that revolution, or even moderate change, were far away in Martinique's future. There was no infrastructure of a radical political movement in the countryside. It was clear that rum served beautifully as the opiate of the masses. You could smell it in the laborer's sweat, in the air of the city's central square and narrow streets. The acrid odor of this light-colored disabling beverage wafted from the open fronts of the bars and restaurants. Rum was dispensed in the cafés clustering in the port area, in the cafés surrounding the Savanne, in the cafés near the market place; it was sold by the bottle in the stores near the Fanons' suburban home; it was available from a street cart next to Fanon's office. Oblivion was never more than fifty feet away in any direction. Fanon wished to work toward the reform of this situation; but in 1952, he couldn't find a place to begin.

He plunged headlong into medical work, giving free attention to the poorest of his brothers who had the sense to consult him at Vauclin. Most of their maladies were due to improper diets and primitive living conditions. The doctor could not avoid the feeling that the essential problems were political and economic rather than medical.

The island needed a restructured society, redistribution of wealth that would provide a better minimum standard of living rather than increased numbers of medical doctors. Fanon became surer of the strongest paragraph that he had composed within the conclusion to *Black Skin, White Masks.* After some reflection on his earlier writing, he said in the last pages, written just before publication:

> I do not carry innocence to the point of believing that appeals to reason or to respect for human dignity can alter reality. For the Negro who works on a sugar plantation in Le Robert, Martinique, there is only one solution: to fight.*

Fanon's mood upon returning to France in 1952 was much the same as it had been in 1943 when he went off to war. Then he had been saturated with fury; he had left the island in order to have a chance to fight against the things that were wrong there. In 1943, though, the situation was clearer; any kind of open action at home would have been suicidal. The enemy in that period was the French navy and the Vichy administration that had been in control of Martinique for three years. In 1940, after France had fallen to Nazi Germany, the French fleet in the Caribbean declared its allegiance to the collaborationist Vichy regime. The British could no longer allow the French freedom of sea action; two large warships were blockaded within the Fort-de-France harbor. Consequently, 5,000 white French sailors descended upon the city's 45,000 inhabitants for a prolonged "Rest and Recreation." Martinique could not digest the influx. The sailors expropriated Fort-de-France's bars, restaurants, hotels, whorehouses, beaches, shops, sidewalks, taxis, and better

Black Skin, White Masks (New York: Grove Press, 1967), p. 224.

apartments. In the summer of 1940, any given sailor had one hundred times the currency in his pockets than the average Martinican had: The military could afford to order the civilians around. The servicemen were rough too; the islanders used to leading peaceful lives. What money failed to do brute power accomplished. Cafés were immediately segregated: black waiters and women, white customers. In the stores sailors expected to be served before Martinicans. At first, segregation came about for economic reasons: With the influx of military money prices went up and the islanders could no longer afford to be customers. By 1941 the sailors were receiving irregular payments because of complications in getting funds from Vichy, but by then the color lines were firmly established. The servicemen weren't going to fraternize with black males. The women were another matter: The white visitors requisitioned them; they considered every young girl on the island a prostitute. Rape often replaced remuneration for those unwilling to conform to the sailors' expectations. The police, used to operating in a colonial environment where blacks were always in the wrong, dismissed rape victims as overpriced prostitutes. In military courts, the navy's word always carried more weight than the Martinicans' complaints. It was a totalitarian racism.

When it began in 1940, Frantz Fanon was fifteen years old, finishing his fourth year at the *lycée*. That summer, M. and Mme. Fanon feared for the safety of their children; they hurried them out of the city to live with an uncle in the countryside. But Frantz and his brothers had to continue with the *lycée;* they were back in Fort-de-France for the fall. He and his brothers lived through three years of the occupation, surviving one small incident after another. A close friend of Fanon's, Marcel Manville, recalls

a time during the first week back in school when the two
of them were walking toward the Savanne, early in the
morning, on their way to class. In the distance, on the
hard-packed dirt of the central square, they saw two sailors kicking a youth lying on the ground. Instinctively they
began to run toward the sailors to try to save the boy's life.
Manville and Fanon were so astounded that they were
without fear; they were able to stop the sailors and inquire
what it was about. The two servicemen stood back and
muttered something about the youth trying to cheat them;
then they left. Fanon and his friend took the badly beaten
youth to the police headquarters for first aid; they explained that he'd been in a fight with other islanders, and
the police fixed him up a bit and released him. The youth
couldn't explain what happened; Fanon and Manville
knew only that they had stopped two hefty sailors from
kicking in the head of a fifteen-year-old. The two students
were later warned that they could have been in serious
trouble for interfering; if there had been other sailors
around they would have been badly beaten themselves;
the police might have arrested them too.

The Vichy regime in Martinique, as represented by the
military, came to mean rape, racism, and rioting. This was
not the France that Fanon had grown up with in school,
but some evil impersonator. His normal reaction, to begin to dislike whites, was sublimated into political curi-
osity. By 1942, the British were helping in this task by
putting the radio-transmitting facilities of their Caribbean colonies at the disposal of the Free French Movement. De Gaulle was clever in propaganda techniques.
When the Americans, in 1943, set up a blockade around
Martinique and Guadeloupe, he blamed the Vichy ad-
ministrations on the islands for the food shortages. De

Gaulle set himself up as the last hope for a recovered
sense of dignity in the Antilles. Pétain and his agents had
destroyed democracy within the empire. The educated
youth in Martinique, like that in certain of the African
colonies, began to respond to the Gaullist message. As
more severe food shortages increased discontent in Fort-
de-France, Fanon, Manville, and their friends looked to
the tall general as the only possible savior for France and
Martinique. Finishing up the first part of the baccalaure-
ate degree in 1943, both Fanon and Manville decided to
join the Caribbean Free French Movement.

They had to act. But they couldn't fight in Martinique
itself because they were greatly outnumbered by the fully
armed regular forces and the Vichy administration
headed by Admiral Georges Robert. Fanon's 1943 military campaign consisted of a guerrilla retreat. The Gaullist troops concealed themselves only so that they might
escape the island by small boat and join one of the larger
Free French camps in British or American territory. Still,
for the seventeen-year-old Fanon it was a courageous
step: parting from a closely knit family, trekking into the
jungle with two of his classmates from the *lycée*, making
contact with the troops; then waiting with them at a beach
on the northern part of Martinique for the small boats that
were ferrying volunteers over to the British island of
Dominica. By the spring of 1943, the number of Martinicans wanting to leave was so great that it was necessary to
stay in hiding near the beach for up to a week. The Vichy
authorities had patrols in the jungle with orders to exter-
minate Gaullist camps. The boat trip itself was dangerous;
the currents in the channel between Dominica and Martinique were viciously strong. According to Manville, the
boats ferrying the men across demanded a fee from each
volunteer as he stepped aboard. They found out later that

certain of the men running the outboard motor crafts were throwing their cargoes overboard halfway across the channel in order to return more swiftly for other fares. Fanon and Manville knew of men who drowned trying to reach Dominica. The ferrying operation was carried out at night to avoid detection by Vichy airplanes.

Life on Dominica was anticlimactic: two months of military training without ever the hint of a battle. There was always the great unseen force in the Caribbean: the United States. All real activity depended on decisions made in Washington. Through 1942, the Roosevelt government sustained the Vichy regime in Fort-de-France with continued deliveries of food and supplies; then in the spring of 1943, in accordance with larger World War II strategies, the United States decided to do away with the collaborators. All that was needed was an embargo on trade with the Antilles; within two months Admiral Georges Robert sued for peace with the Americans, or rather with the Gaullists acting on behalf of the United States. One thousand Free French troops made a peaceful invasion from Dominica. Frantz Fanon was in one of the boats crowded with chanting and yelling patriots; many of them felt as if they had won the war. Henri Hoppenot, the new High Commissioner for the Antilles, announced the restoration of the French Republic in Martinique. Speaking from a high, wooden platform in the center of the Savanne, on Bastille Day, 1943, Hoppenot stated that he was sure that 95 per cent of the population would be relieved to be able to switch its allegiance to the "legitimate" head of state of France, Charles de Gaulle. After the municipal band, recently declared part of the Free French Movement, had played "The Marseillaise," Fanon, packed tightly with the other troops into the center of the city, heard Hoppenot read a telegram from the general:

The French Committee of National Liberation is happy to welcome into the French Empire the patriotic people of Martinique and Guadeloupe united for resistance and for the liberation of the national territory. I know how long you have wanted to join us to carry on the war against France's enemies. . . . I have no doubt that by your effort and discipline, cohesion and will to serve, you will be worthy of the love that the mother country bears toward the French Antilles.

The crowd applauded wildly at the news of the triumph—the return to the arms of the true mother country. The age of decolonization had not yet dawned in the French empire of the Americas.

Admiral Robert noted bitterly in his memoirs:

> . . . the idea had spread across the island that General de Gaulle was a black general wanting, like Toussaint L'Ouverture, to free the colored peoples from the yoke of the white land owners.*

He wasn't quite accurate; the political sophistication of the Martinicans was not so far advanced. The hostility toward Vichy was never directed against the island's property owners. Not even Fanon thought much about the color of Charles de Gaulle. He and his comrades were reacting to an immediate situation: the brutality of the visiting French troops. These sailors, to the Martinicans' way of thinking, were not really French, but closer to the Nazi forces that were occupying most of the *patrie*. Fanon never recorded his own feelings in the summer of 1943; but his actions speak loudly enough. After Hoppenot's Bastille Day celebration, he along with Manville and a

* *La France aux Antilles de 1939 à 1943* (Paris: Plon, 1950), p. 28.

third close friend volunteered for active duty in the regular French army for the duration of the Second World War. Fanon was still in a mood to fight; he had been led to believe that Germany was the only great enemy.

II
The Mother Country

Growing up in Fort-de-France, and in the Second World War, Fanon had two close friends, Manville and Mosole. Mosole was a mulatto with a complexion made even paler by constant preoccupation with ill health. A strong athlete who survived the rigors of war beautifully, he was ever convinced that he would succumb to an impending sickness. He once went so far as to specify it: tuberculosis. There were no signs of it in those days, but in the late 1950s, in France, he had to enter a sanatorium for the disease. He has remained there since. Mosole was well-informed and cynical; by 1943 he knew everything about racism and exploitation, but had calmly decided to go ahead with a professional career, make money, and enjoy what he could in life. Manville, six-feet-two-inches tall and two hundred pounds, was the son of one of the three socialists in Martinique; the elder Manville was the island's *défenseur officieux*—because of his superior education he had been given authority to defend the poor blacks in lower courts without pay. His son determined early in life to become a lawyer too; he felt compelled to speak for just causes regardless of his own title or the odds against his case; he was defending other students, before higher authorities, even in the *lycée*. In courtrooms, living rooms, restaurants, cars—wherever there are other people— Manville always loved to talk. A key word dropped in front of him excites him into a continually expanding monologue rolling backward or forward over ten-year stretches of experiences. He will pause, raising his eyes as high as possible, a gesture that appears necessary to lay bare each ample reservoir of anecdotes, statistics, tastes, smells, visions, and opinions. He has a successful practice today defending civil servants against the government; there is a lot of money in this kind of law which allows Manville to give his services without charge to a huge number of left-wing causes. He often describes himself as a Communist; but the C.P. confiscated his card because of his unorthodox political activities. Manville feels a bit embarrassed at not being a "card-carrying Communist," says one of his friends, but he is confident that the party will catch up with him soon. It is difficult to catch Manville, though; he has a thick calendar date-book in his suit pocket filled with his obligations to radical meetings, exploited workers, and underdeveloped territories. He is already busy into the next decade.

In 1944, the *S.S. Oregon* transporting Manville, Mosole, and Fanon from the Antilles to North Africa was over-crowded with black volunteers. The voyage took almost a month; the three slept on deck under a makeshift canvas shelter; the space below was impossibly packed with sick human beings. Mosole knew that all of this would ruin his health. It was not that the food was bad; it might have been, but there wasn't enough of it to allow one the luxury of repulsion. Everyone was on miniscule rations from the beginning of the voyage in order that there wouldn't be a hunger riot toward the end. One morning as they were drying themselves after a wet, cold, sleepless night, Fanon looked about him at the bedraggled black troops, then upward toward the bridge where the self-satisfied white officers were strolling about. He tapped the shivering Mosole on the shoulder. Fanon pointed back toward the fluttering tricolor and muttered, "It should be replaced with a huge black flag." For the first time, the three of them talked about how their ancestors originally arrived in the Antilles. One jokingly announced his refusal to disembark south of the Sahara.

There was only this kind of humor to smooth over in-creasing tensions during the voyage. A crisis developed out of the officers' attempts to requisition the "services" of a group of female volunteers from Martinique and Guadeloupe—WACs as we would call them. The troops were furious seeing the officers consorting with their women; Manville described the situation as building up toward a race riot. The three friends were not themselves upset at the prospect of the seduction of the WACs; but they did have to revise some of their earlier assumptions where they had dealt with the Vichy troops as separate from the French army.

They reached Casablanca before there was any serious

violence. The French were securely in control of
Morocco, but the Martinican troops were sent southward
anyway to be stationed in Guercif, a low-lying area of the
Atlas Mountains. The town has a climate similar to the
Sahara's; the temperature goes up to 140 degrees Faren-
heit on a summer day and will plummet to below freezing
in the night. Fanon, though, never bothered to talk about
the weather; he was thoroughly absorbed in the new racial
and social tensions of North Africa. It took several weeks
to sort out the five cliques and levels of life at Guercif:
Fanon's analyses were worked out orally with the aid of
Manville and Mosole, both of whom had caught the virus
of their friend's sociological voyeurism. Fanon did carry
a notebook around with him, but he hated to write; he was
at his best during heated conversations or even argu-
ments.

Fanon observed within the troops stationed at Guercif
that there were noticeable barriers between the French
from the metropolitan territory and the settlers in North
Africa; both groups, though, looked down on the Moslems in the army, who didn't care for the blacks. Fanon's
company of soldiers, from Martinique, held aloof from
the African troops, especially the Senegalese. One would
think that color line would have been the clearest factor
of separation; but the situation was more complex. There
were special rations given to the Africans—vegetable
crops harvested in West Africa. The Antilleans were allowed European food. Sometimes the supplies were so
low, however, that all of the soldiers were treated to the
local delicacy of dried camel skin.

During the two months in Guercif there was about as
much military action as there had been in Dominica. Although Fanon and his friends were getting a good social
education, it was hardly enough to make up for the 140-

degree days, camel-skin lunches, and total lack of excitement. One day a M. Darnal showed up in the camp as a representative of the Gaullist coalition running the French war effort. The commanding officers hurried the three hundred troops into parade formation for Darnal's inspection. The visitor, as each company paused before his reviewing stand, inquired of the troops if there were any complaints or questions. Out of the three hundred soldiers that passed by that afternoon only three hands were raised. Monsieur Darnal made an appointment to meet with Fanon, Manville, and Mosole to speak with them privately.

The commanding officers of the base intercepted the three on their way to Darnal's headquarters. Fanon, Manville, and Mosole had two interviews that day, and both of them, to their way of thinking, were rather enjoyable. Manville, of course, gave counsel on how to handle the first ordeal: "Don't say a thing," he told the other two in Creole patois as they were hurried inside. They stood stony-faced and close-mouthed as four officers tried to find out what they would complain about to the visitor. The white officers got more and more excited while the black servicemen refused to talk; the superiors would have loved to threaten punishment, but that would have ruined their chances with Darnal. After the questions came hints of rewards for the three if they gave a good report. Manville was using all his strength not to giggle; he always enjoyed laughing. Especially when he looked at Fanon, the most ferocious-looking soldier imaginable.

They met the Gaullist representative in a serious frame of mind, knowing their responsibility to the troops too timid to complain. They described the worst facets of life at Guercif, emphasizing the different kinds of racism and the lack of being able to contribute to the war effort.

Three days later, the three hundred troops were transferred out of southern Morocco into Algeria, one step closer to the fighting. Fanon and his friends, now stationed in Bougie, on the Mediterranean coast, found new entertainment—an officers' training school with students selected almost exclusively from the French haute bourgeoisie. The three began to get a feeling for class structure without ever having looked at Marx.

The cumulative effect of the voyage from Martinique, the stay at Guercif, and watching the practiced snobbery of the officer candidates at Bougie was anger. The three Martinicans expressed their distaste for the new life through a disorganized kind of rebellion, and by picking on each other. Fanon, for instance, refused to go out at night alone: He always wanted somebody to talk to and with whom to record his observations. But he didn't have the courage to make new friends; it had to be Manville or Mosole. One night, finally, he had to go to the movies alone because the other two absolutely refused to continue to follow his lead. He came back at 9 P.M. all in a lather about the film, which he claimed was centered about the jazz and jazz musicians whom the other two always enjoyed. Mosole and Manville were so excited at his wild descriptions that they hurried out to catch the last showing. The film had nothing to do with jazz; it was an abominably boring love story. The two returned to the barracks to see if Fanon was all right; they honestly believed that the new life had become too much for him and that he had suffered some sort of breakdown. There he was, waiting, roaring with laughter, happy at having imposed on his friends: He had been swindled by the movie house—why not they too?

Another kind of rebellion was a competition among them to earn the worst possible military record at Bougie without actually going to jail. The three were famous on the post. Again it was Manville who knew how to keep them out of prison while advising them on which rules might be broken with the most spectacular repercussions. Recently Manville said, "You should have seen our records; they went on for pages and pages listing the minor infractions. . . ." He rolled his eyes, laughed, then continued:

> In the early summer of 1944, they pulled us all together in Bougie and some colonel announced that there was going to be an allied invasion of southern Europe. The French army was going to protect the left flank moving northward into Europe. There was bound to be some rough fighting. The first contingent of French troops would be volunteers. Who wanted to fight?

In Bougie, that afternoon, there were only three volunteers. The noncommissioned officers were first amazed and then relieved that the three great troublemakers would soon be leaving.

Fanon enjoyed dramatic situations; but he was also troubled and angry by the time he embarked for Europe. He and his comrades had marched across a desolate and poverty-stricken area of the world. The Germans, retreating from North Africa, had stripped the countryside clean. Livestock, wheat, fruits, vegetables and dry goods had all been transferred to Nazi strongholds in Europe. By 1944 food and fuel were severely rationed everywhere. An American war correspondent mentioned that only one hotel in all of North Africa had hot water, the once elegant Algiers Aletti that burned furniture in its hot-water heaters to provide the luxury of sixty minutes each morning. The Americans shipped supplies to the area, but demanded payment in the form of promissory notes from the provisional French government that handled the distribution of the food and clothing. It became a commercial venture; only the Europeans with a bit of money of their own benefited from the American aid. Elsewhere there was famine and disease; Moslem children died by the scores. Fanon's confused feelings about racial subtleties disappeared before the hard realities of the wretched of Algeria. It was far worse than anything he had seen in the Caribbean. In Oran, Fanon had to watch French soldiers tossing crusts of bread to Moslem children fighting each other for the food. In Bougie, he went into a rage when he came upon Moslem children picking through military garbage. He suddenly went after the five- and six-year-olds, threatening to kill them if they didn't get out of the garbage; Fanon returned quietly to Manville and Moselle, who wondered if he was in his right mind. No one said anything about the incident, but it was this kind of helpless despair which made them all the more anxious to cross into Europe.

In August, 1944, eight hundred British and American warships carried the allied forces into a first assault on the Côte d'Azur. Fanon and his friends were part of the Ninth Division of Colonial Infantry, First French Army, which disembarked at the Bay of Saint-Tropez and moved toward Marseilles. It was a mopping-up action involving little direct contact with the Germans. One night, after his company had turned northward from Toulon, Fanon had just been relieved from sentry duty when he heard a burst of machine-gun fire. Everyone was back on his feet, rifles ready; Fanon's replacement was dead. German scouts had killed him and disappeared into the moonless night.

The Ninth Division pushed northward into the grape-growing hills along the Rhone River. The main Allied drive had advanced ahead of them and to the east; there was nothing to slow French progress. Fanon and his friends were marching twenty to thirty miles a day; their first wounds of the war were their feet. They had covered three hundred miles of roadway before the first heavy action northeast of Lyons. Even in battle racial issues could interfere with combat efficiency. Toward Dijon a well-placed German machine-gun nest stopped the easy advance of the French. A Senegalese company was ordered into action against the Germans; three times the Africans were thrown back with heavy losses. Fanon heard one of the Senegalese soldiers muttering, "Why don't the *Toubabs* go into action?" At that moment, Fanon assumed that he was a *Toubab,* or European. After the firing subsided, he knew this was absurd; despite the fact that the Martinicans had been awarded Western rations at Guercif, the Europeans, in other important matters, classified them as "natives" too.

The confusion was quite natural. As a child Fanon had heard incredible tales about the fierceness of the African, more particularly, the Senegalese warrior. When Fanon was thirteen years old a regiment of Senegalese soldiers had visited Martinique:

> All I knew about them was what I had heard from the veterans of the First World War: "They attack with the bayonet, and, when that doesn't work, they just punch their way through the machine-gun fire with their fists. . . . They cut off heads and collect human ears.*

The thirteen-year-old Fanon had gone out to scour the streets of Fort-de-France for a glimpse of the savages. His father had told him of the Africans' red scarves and belts;

Black Skin, White Masks, p. 162.

when M. Fanon, who worked in the French customs, was able to procure two of the scarves, the whole family gathered around the objects with veneration. Fanon had a teacher in grammar school who entertained the class with fantastic tales of the Senegalese in battle. He described their weird trances during peaceful interludes, when the Africans turned to prayer. On Saturday afternoons, at this period in his life, Fanon's greatest treat was to be sent to the local movie house, which featured Tarzan epics. The audience, quite naturally, identified with the white hero battling the darker forces of African evil.

In the fall of 1944, to add to the racial mystifications, the white command decided to classify the Martinicans within the Ninth Division as *Toubabs* too. East of Dijon, as the fall temperatures fell toward the freezing mark, orders went out to "bleach" the Division. The Africans were to be sent back to the south of France; they could not be expected to continue to function in the cold weather. The Antilleans, though, were left in the north; it didn't matter that the climate in Martinique and Guadeloupe was tropical too. Manville commented later that the shifting of troops seemed to be based on the criterion of assimilation—those who were more fluent in French were expected to resist lower temperatures.

By November, Fanon and Manville shared Mosole's cynicism about these matters. In each town that they had passed as they moved upward from the Midi, there had been liberation balls, huge dances, and dinners to welcome the French troops. In the small villages, the white women even feared to touch a black hand, to say nothing of dancing with a Martinican. It was Manville who recalled that in Toulon, during one of the larger liberation celebrations, the three of them watched French women dancing with Italian war prisoners—the same women who had turned down requests to dance from black French servicemen.

With the Senegalese departed for their vacation on the Côte d'Azur, the fighting became more intense in and around the city of Besançon. Fanon, Manville, and Mosole were in different regiments; each morning, though, they would try to get word to each other that they were alive and unwounded. Fanon did get a very minor wound in November; the idea that he could be grazed by a German bullet seemed to infuriate him; he went back to action with almost an insane energy. He was always testing himself, pushing to the severest limits; then he would go slightly further—to see what would happen. The first injury assured him that he could be braver, endure more pain, fight harder, and ignore racial insults. In the heavily wooded valley of the Doubs River, east of Besançon, his regiment came under heavy counterattack; the men dug into defensive positions, but soon artillery supplies were threateningly low. Fanon volunteered to head a small party that would bring up ammunition to the forward positions. During the mission he was badly injured by mortar shrapnel in the chest and shoulder.

Fanon had a two-month convalescence at the military hospital of Nantua, northeast of Lyons. Toward the end, he became too restless to be kept inside the hospital. He secretly began to play some soccer with a local team against a Lyons team; he also built some friendships, male and female, in the nearby city. In February, 1945, Colonel Raoul Salan, Commander of the Sixth Regiment of Colonial Infantry, personally awarded Frantz Fanon the *Croix de guerre avec étoile de bronze* for his "brilliant conduct during the operations in the valley of the Doubs."* Fanon

*The decoration ceremony became one of the more ironic memories in Fanon's later career. At the same time that he was becoming a

was then promoted to corporal. So that by the time he was ready to go home, some of the bitterest feelings had mellowed. He was a decorated veteran of almost two years of warfare; he had a right to be French and wanted to be French—if only to help begin the reform of his society. Manville, also decorated with the *Croix de guerre,* also promoted to corporal, felt the same way. Corporal Mosole, wearing the third *Croix de guerre* on the ship plowing toward the southern Caribbean, remained cynical.

Frantz and Joby Fanon based their hopes for a better society on Aimé Césaire, running as the Communist Party's parliamentary candidate from Martinique in the first election of the Fourth Republic. Césaire came from the same middle-class background as the Fanons but had escaped the island at an early age for an education at the Lycée Louis le Grand in Paris, and the Sorbonne. Thrown in the midst of France's African intellectuals, he "became African himself." James Baldwin, watching Césaire speak at a Conference of Black Writers and Artists, described him as

> a caramel-colored individual with a tendency toward roundness and smoothness. . . . All this changes the moment he begins to speak. It becomes at once apparent that his curious, slow-moving blandness is related to the grace and patience of a jungle cat and that the intelligence behind those spectacles is of a very penetrating and demagogic order.*

revolutionary within the Algerian war, Salan took charge of the French forces in North Africa. Salan eventually headed the fascist *Organisation Armée Secrète* dedicated to destroying all of Algeria rather than accept the rule of the Moslem majority there.
*James Baldwin, *Nobody Knows My Name* (New York: Dial, 1961), p. 32.

Césaire had been at the head of a group of intellectual refugees from the Antilles who put out their own review in Paris, *Légitime Défense,* with articles dissecting all aspects of Caribbean colonial society. Earlier than Fanon, he despaired of these islands where the blacks treated each other as "dirty niggers." Martinique, he said, was the bastard of Europe and Africa, dripping with self-hatred. Yet he had returned—to seek a political solution to the cultural desolation. The Communists, Césaire felt, could begin to renovate Martinique's economic infrastructure; a more healthy society might develop. He tried in his own future, and that of the islands, with the very bright prospects of the French C.P. emerging from its dominant position within the World War II Resistance.

That Frantz Fanon worked for Césaire's election in 1946 indicates not that the former was a confirmed Marxist at this early time, or a revolutionary, but only that Fanon felt that things were not quite as perfect as they might be within the French republic, or in Martinique. Still, this first political endeavor was instructive; he began to think about the mechanics of social change in agricultural areas. Joby Fanon was able to show his younger brother certain weaknesses of Césaire's first campaign. The candidate never reached the real countryside but contented himself with giving speeches in larger villages and towns across the island. The Fanons learned the difficulties of trying to reach the peasants: Joby describes the intense suspicions of the country people whom they encountered on the trip; they couldn't even begin conversations until they had firmly established their own identity as islanders. The 1946 excursion, which had originally been planned so that they could listen to the fine oratory of Césaire, and aid him when possible, led to quite different patterns of thought: Joby Fanon today continues to study agrarian problems in the Antilles and is convinced that any serious changes in Latin American societies will come in response to pressures from rurally based forces.*

A decade after the Césaire campaign, Frantz Fanon wrote:

> Thus from the capital city they [the nationalist parties] will "parachute" organizers into the villages who are either unknown or too young, and who, armed with instructions from the central authority, mean to treat . . . the village like a factory cell. . . . The makers of the future nation's history trample unconcernedly over small local disputes. . . . The old men, surrounded by respect in all traditional societies and usually invested with unquestionable moral authority, are publicly held up to ridicule. The occupying power's local authorities do not fail to use the resentment thus engendered, and keep in touch with the slightest decisions adopted by this caricature of authority. Police repression, well-informed because it is based on precise information, strikes. The parachuted leaders and the consequential members of the new assembly are arrested.†

The Wretched of the Earth is a refining of some of the earlier Martinican experiences in light of the Algerian war. It is Fanon warning against one of the blunders exposed in the diary of Che Guevara—the idea that an outsider will immediately be welcomed as a savior by the oppressed peoples of rural areas.

After the Second World War, Fanon's education progressed in other directions. In 1946 he was back in the

*See J. Fanon, "Autonomie et économie des Antilles," *Bulletin de liaison du Centre socialiste de documentation et d'études sur les problèmes du Tiers Monde* (May, 1969).
† *The Wretched of the Earth* (New York: Grove Press, 1968), p. 113.

lycée; he wanted to be able to go on to a university. The teachers in Fort-de-France who remember Fanon are those he had in this later period. Certain of the professors know of him because of his career; one of them, though, had no idea of what had happened to his pupil, but he recalled that he was *"un jeune homme très sérieux,"* aloof from the other students mostly because of the intensity of his concentration on academic matters. It was in this period that he was reading Nietzsche, Karl Jaspers, Kierkegaard, and Hegel. He was particularly impressed with the new works of Jean-Paul Sartre; he began to think about a career in drama.

In 1947, Fanon's father died; the family was hard-pressed financially. Frantz had won a scholarship to a university in a field of his choosing. Politics and drama seemed luxuries at that moment; he had to be more practical. He wanted a career where he could be of use on the island; medicine would have been ideal, but he had lost too much time in the war; it would take too many years. He turned to his friends Manville and Mosole, who were also planning to continue their studies at a metropolitan university, Manville in law. Mosole came up with the ideal solution: dentistry! It was a socially useful occupation, but more important for Mosole, there was money in it. For one time in his life, Fanon settled for the liberal compromise: He departed for Paris with his two comrades to become a dentist.

After three weeks of introductory courses in dental school, Fanon showed up in Manville's room with his suitcase packed, ready to depart for Lyons. The friend was totally astounded. Before he could ask why, Fanon commented, "There are just too many niggers in Paris."

Manville agreed that this was something of a drawback,

but still, he could use more of an explanation. Fanon then explained that he had never met so many idiots in his life as in dentistry school. He couldn't tolerate it. It was worse than the *S.S. Oregon,* as boring as Guercif. He would rather go back to Bougie or the Valley of the Doubs.

Manville tried to stop the tirade by asking why he had chosen Lyons and what he was going to do there. Fanon had decided to take the year's preparation in chemistry, physics, and biology necessary before entering medical school. He thought he could live more cheaply in the provinces. He had friends around Lyons from his soccer days at the Hospital of Nantua. Seeing Fanon off at the Gare Saint Lazare, Manville was relieved that he had chosen law.

In ordinary times, Lyons is a fat city. Standing at the juncture of the Saône and Rhone rivers, it is the crossroads of a major part of the commerce among France and Italy and Switzerland. Lyons has learned how to make traveling merchants stop there for a day or two by providing what most gourmets consider the finest food in Europe. Whereas the richer businessmen can be carried out of small restaurants that cater to the most exotic and refined palates, the middle class, and once in a while the students, crowd into the city's larger cafés that have mastered the art of providing edible food for huge numbers of people. The Brasserie Georges, sucking in hungry passengers from the railroad terminal, seats five hundred persons at a time. One of its supervising chefs watches over the preparation of gallons of sauces for thousands of platters of veal, chicken, and fish; another is in charge only of sauerkraut and pork products. The Brasserie's food is of such high quality that people descend from trains for the sole purpose of a meal there.

Besides food, the city makes silk. When Fanon arrived there 10 per cent of Lyons' half-million population worked for the silk industry. This region of France lives off Europe's ability to indulge itself in the finest luxuries: When the continent thinks about tightening its belt, Lyons shrivels and toughens. It is then that the laborers—even the waiters from the Brasserie Georges—reappear from behind the gaudy façades of Second-Empire architecture; it is then that the city re-establishes its other reputation for hard radicalism. In 1830, the silk workers' strike in Lyons anticipated the turmoil and revolution in the rest of the nation; in 1836 there was a longer and more violent strike in this Department of the Rhone. Whereas historians have always looked to Paris as a barometer of left-wing pressures in the country, Lyons too should have this reputation. A general strike in Lyons in 1848 preceded the revolution in Paris; there was also a communist commune ruling Lyons in 1870. In 1968, the University of Lyons was shut down by students before the Sorbonne in Paris.

The Second World War left all of France just skin and bones; the Lyonnaise workers of 1947 were as militant as those of a century before. In Paris, the Gaullists were struggling to keep the country from the rule of the Communists, who had a legitimate claim to power as the majority force within the Resistance. Premier Ramadier had sent Georges Bidault to Washington to get emergency aid; without it, he warned, "The large cities of France will be without bread in February." The month in which Fanon arrived in Paris and left for Lyons there were strikes by the coal miners, the chemicals workers, the electrical workers, the beet-sugar growers, train engineers; Peugeot, Simca, and Citroen workers; construction workers, concierges, and metro conductors. As Fanon arrived in Lyons, laborers were occupying the silk works and metallurgical complexes.

The Minister of Education, trying to catch up with the revolution, had nationalized some of the nation's larger, and better-known, houses of prostitution and turned them over to the students, but in Lyons funds for the conversion of bordellos into dormitories never came through. Fanon and the other students slept in small cubicles that had been the prostitutes' working quarters—with bed, sink, and ornate bidet. The students could work in the central lounge with its high ceilings, eight-foot mirrors, dark paneling, red leather divans, and gas lighting fixtures that had been half converted into electrical outlets with bare bulbs. The city was exploding with political tensions—sporadic warfare between the newly created state police (created by the Socialist Party as part of its war against Communism) and militant workers—all of which added to the bizarreness of things for one recently arrived from a quiet Caribbean island.

Fanon had a ten-minute walk from his five-story home on the narrow rue Tupin, across the broad, green expanse of the Rhone River, to classes at the Faculté des Sciences. The Faculté de Médicine was further toward the suburbs on the very wide Boulevard Rockefeller. The students were unionized into the General Students Association with headquarters in an older, narrower, darker part of town, where there were facilities for meetings and editing political publications. By their numbers, the students controlled this *quartier;* and Fanon enjoyed life in the cafés around the place Guichard before his work became too carefully organized to allow for casual student social-life. In 1947 and 1948 his political engagements threatened his academic career: He was always involved in debates, going to left-wing meetings, touring occupied factories.

Things were made easier by a special 1947 law exempting all army veterans from academic examinations; Fanon could go on to medical school without showing the gaps left in his scientific education by too keen a sense of politics.

Of Lyons' four hundred university students less than twenty were black—all male and mostly from West Africa. There was a pitifully small black community in the city, and no eligible black women of Fanon's age. There was no choice but to live in a white world, and that, at first, was difficult. Not even the city's prostitutes wanted black clients. Except for one Fanon found who confided she wanted him *because* he was black. She later admitted that she had had an orgasm the first time before he had begun sexual intercourse.

Within student circles Fanon found women who would accept him as a human being: One with whom he had an affair became pregnant. It had not been a drawn-out affair, or what the French call a *liaison,* but the girl thought she was in love with Fanon. He wasn't sure of his own feelings; in fact, he was so upset that he had to get on a train for Paris to spill out his troubles to closer friends. Fanon, at this point, was not sure that he liked Europe or wanted to be married to a European: Manville advised him that there was no legal necessity for marriage—only for support of the child. Joby Fanon emphasized, too, that his brother had a moral obligation toward the child; the mother was quite capable of taking care of herself. His brother and friend both advised Fanon that a forced marriage would be the worst solution of all—and, essentially, that was the advice he wanted. There were other women in Lyons to whom he felt closer than the mother of his child. After Frantz Fanon's death, Joby Fanon brought the daughter, a student in Paris, back to Martinique to meet her grandmother; he felt his brother would have appreciated this. . . .

Fanon's surroundings—the whorehouse dormitory, and raging political debates—did nothing to soothe his psyche during the pregnancy ordeal. A Lyons lawyer recalls that they would stay up all night in the unconverted bordello giving prolonged critiques of existentialism, utopian socialism, and sex. One of the students there, after a whole night of discussions, tried to commit suicide by jumping out of his fifth-floor cubicle window to prove some obscure point. Still, Fanon managed to have a steadily improving record in medical school: His teachers had great respect for him, and came to treat him almost as a colleague. One professor, Dr. Marcel Colin, a specialist in the legal aspects of psychiatric care, considered Fanon one of the best students at the university. Colin would occasionally invite Fanon to dinner with his family at their medieval château in the low hills to the west of the city. The doctor had that easy kind of self-confidence that flows from the combination of every kind of personal success and security. He was a leftist too, having edited a clandestine newspaper in Paris during the Resistance. With Fanon he had the relaxed kind of relationship he would have had with any other white student whose intelligence and politics impressed him; and Fanon responded accordingly. Yet one evening, when Fanon had left the small château after a long dinner, Colin confessed to his wife that he feared the student. Observing him performing an autopsy earlier that day, Colin had seen a glint in Fanon's eyes: The professor had found himself retreating a few steps from Fanon's scalpel. But also, Colin noticed that Fanon's right hand trembled terribly when it approached the cadaver; he would never make a decent surgeon.

To relieve his own tensions during this period, Fanon began to write plays: *Parallel Hands, The Drowning Eye,* and *The Conspiracy.* One can generalize that they were leftist existential works; one can speculate that they were highly melodramatic and not suitable for publication; and one knows that Fanon grew away from them and preferred that they remain buried. That he had reached the depths of depression somewhere in the middle years of his medical education becomes evident anyway in *Black Skin, White Masks,* composed in uneven spurts of energy in the same period that he began and finished his career as a dramatist. After 1948 in Lyons there were times when he felt

> battered down by tom-toms, cannibalism, intellectual deficiency, fetishism, racial defects, and above all else, above all: "Sho' good eatin.'"*

Filled with shame and self-hatred, Fanon turned away from the white world, where if someone liked him, it was made clear that it was not because of his color, or if they hated him, they had to qualify the hatred with disclaimers of racial prejudice. But his black brothers rejected him too; they had become almost white; they were going to have white wives and very light brown children. Little by little, their status would improve. They didn't really need black friends. . . .

> I came into this world with the desire to give order to things [Fanon said at this point in his life], my one great hope was to be of the world; and then I discovered that I was only an object among other objects.
> Sealed into that crushing objecthood, I turned beseechingly to others. Their attention was a liberation . . . endowing me once more with an agility that I had

Black Skin, White Masks, p. 112.

thought lost. . . . But just as I reached the other side, I stumbled, and the movements, the attitudes, the glances of the other fixed me there. . . . I was indignant; I demanded an explanation. Nothing happened. I burst apart. Now the fragments have been put together by another self.*

It was in this period of deep confusion that Fanon's education in existentialism took its shape from Karl Jaspers, the German philosopher whose classic work, *General Psychopathology,* had run to seven editions between 1913 and 1959, when he died. Jaspers maintained that "man becomes conscious of his innerself only in border situations," severe depressions, or even nervous breakdowns. After such a "border situation," man regenerates himself "never through knowledge alone, but only through his relations with others." Fanon had reached a "border situation" when he wrote:

Yesterday, awakening to the world, I saw the sky turn upon itself utterly and wholly. I wanted to rise, but the disemboweled silence fell back upon me, its wings paralyzed. Without responsibility, straddling Nothingness and Infinity, I began to weep.†

Out of the fragmented despair of these early years at Lyons, Fanon was able to rebuild an actional, functional, and creative personality. His poetic introspection gave way to serious medical research; the existential torment disappeared before positive political programs. The depression melted away as his work became of greater importance to him than his race.

Ibid., p. 109.
†*Ibid.*, p. 140.

Interruptions . . . .

In November, 1951, Frantz Fanon defended his medical thesis before a board of five professors. The student's work, *Troubles mentaux et syndromes psychiatriques dans L'Héré-do-dégénération-spino-cérébelleuse. Un Cas de Maladie de Frie-dreich avec délire de possession,* was a conventional piece of neurological research except for the fact that it began with a quote from Nietzsche's *Thus Spake Zarathustra* express-ing Fanon's own dedication to the living world rather than to petrified scholarship. During the defense, Fanon refused to accept the criticisms of the two doctors who were hostile to the work; instead he parried them with masses of statistical information about the nervous syndrome that was the subject of his research. Drowned by the student's torrents of data, the two critics, by the end of the two-hour defense, grudgingly conceded that with one or two minor changes Fanon's thesis would be entirely acceptable. Fanon had completed all the requirements for becoming a medical doctor. He had already begun to practice psychotherapy, under guidance, at the Hôpital de Saint-Ylie outside of Lyons. He would continue on with a psychiatric residency after a vacation in Martinique, and a chance to see his family.

By 1951 Fanon had pulled himself out of the introspective paralysis described in *Black Skin, White Masks.* His career was going well; he was writing, and his political energies were flowing into more clearly defined channels. He was very much involved with someone new, Josie Dublé, a white woman, slightly younger than he, from a socialist background, but not particularly politicized herself. He had first met her in 1948 while she was still a student at a *lycée* at Lyons. Josie was an extremely intense person, strikingly attractive, with long black hair and a smooth, tan complexion. She helped Fanon greatly by taking dictation at home. He wasn't manually dexterous; his handwriting was often illegible and he didn't know how to type. He needed someone to keep up with his thoughts. In hospital work all his notes were dictated to nurses; after he and Josie were married in 1952, she continued to assist him with manuscripts. Later on, when they moved to North Africa, they had a son whom they named Olivier.

Fanon never tried to deny his own racial origins. While in medical school he helped to organize the Union of Students from Overseas France in Lyons, and he put out a newspaper, *Tam-Tam* (the French pronunciation of tom-

tom). The name was inspired by the recurring image of the tom-tom in Aimé Césaire's play, *Larmes miraculeuses.* The blacks in Lyons were going to establish their own identity in the face of perpetual insinuations from the whites: The tom-tom had served as an effective means of long-distance communication before Samuel Morse was born. But for some reason, the newspaper never got off the ground: Only one issue was printed with Fanon doing most of the writing. The quality of the writing, however, impressed the city's academics; Fanon was invited as a guest lecturer at the Lycée du Parc. His talk there on black poetry moved one of the professors, a M. Achille, to award him what he considered the highest possible tribute: "In the end," said the professor, "you are white." Fanon became sensitive about praise. He didn't get along well with the leftist philosophy professor, Francis Jeanson, one of the first readers of the manuscript of *Black Skin, White Masks,* simply because Jeanson thought the essays were brilliant. Fanon felt he was implying that the work was amazing for a black man.

In 1952 Fanon returned to the countryside of central France, near the city of Mende; he had been admitted to the residency program at the Hôpital de Saint-Alban under Professor François Tosquelles. At the time, this doctor and his hospital were the model for numerous psychiatric reform projects within all of France. Tosquelles is a short, nervous man who speaks with a pronounced Spanish accent after more than two decades of living in France. When someone notices the accent, or asks him to repeat a word, he begins to enunciate the language (smiling a bit with each syllable), as though he were in a beginner's phonetics class. Tosquelles' students are very fond of, and loyal to, this man who came from

Barcelona, studied in Paris, and was a political refugee after the Spanish Civil War. Tosquelles' name is synonymous with *thérapeutique institutionnelle,* which might best be translated as "communal therapy." Yet this is not a sufficient explanation of the French term. Tosquelles wrote:

> . . . psychiatry cannot be reduced to a vision of man as just another variety of living organism. Psychiatry is a medical activity which must be based on a "total" or "anthropological" view of man including, at the same time, that which we would call the biological, the psychological, historic, and sociologic perspectives.*

Tosquelles reluctantly accepted the fact that there was a necessity for psychiatric hospitals in modern Western society, but he wanted to revolutionize the concept of what the hospital is, as well as get patients out of institutions and back into the community as rapidly as possible. For him, the hospital itself would function as a community not only with doctors and nurses working to cure patients, but patients themselves helping each other; and even maintenance personnel and administrators would be included within the mechanism of the cure.

> Psychiatry [Tosquelles explained at a 1953 medical conference], forced by society to be isolated with its patients behind the walls of asylums, cannot remain blind to the relationships between mental illnesses, the personality, the place, and the actual events lived through.
>
> Psychiatry must define itself by its efforts at inte-

---

* *Le Travail thérapeutique à l'hôpital psychiatrique* (Paris: Editions du Scarabée, 1967), p. 7.

grating medical and organic knowledge with the concrete psychology of the patients.*

It was a materialistic psychiatry with great emphasis on
even the smaller details of the structure of the mental
institution. At Saint-Alban, group therapy was more than
an occasional interlude; it was the patients' way of life.
The hospital was divided into "quarters" and then smaller
groups of patients who lived together, worked with each
other, and attempted, at least in the later stages of the
cure, to help each other. It was a delicate operation; Tosquelles was interested in every facet, always modifying
details to see whether something would work better, always trying a number of different "cures" on long-term
patients.

Tosquelles wrote on the details of organizing *ergothérapie*, which was the term he used to describe work therapy
thoroughly integrated within hospital communal life. He
wanted his students to take account of:

1. The structure, density, homogeneity of the groups
   of patients involved in the work.
2. The type of work the patients would be doing.
3. The systems of completing the work.
4. All of the materials to be used.
5. The kind of social atmosphere that the work itself
   would create.
6. The degree of specialization needed to complete
   each aspect of the work.
7. The degree of collaboration needed to complete
   the work.
8. The extent of the responsibility that should be ex-

*Congrès des médecins aliénistes et neurologues de France et des
pays de langue française (Pau, 1953).

pected of the workers in order to carry on their tasks.*

Psychiatrists working with the Spanish doctor had to be structuralists as well as therapists; they were required to analyze the minutest details of everyday routines.

Tosquelles and his students continually used the term *thérapeutique institutionnelle;* at a medical congress he was asked to elaborate on this concept. The doctor answered that fourteen years of experiments at Saint-Alban had allowed him and his students to draw up certain guide-lines as to how they wanted to organize psychiatric institutions. Hospitals would be divided up into different *quartiers* of nurses, patients, and doctors, within these there would be communities of no more than ten to twelve patients living and working together. The doctors had a responsibility to train nurses in the handling of groups; the nurses too would keep detailed notes on each individual patient. There would be a full schedule of meetings between doctors and nurses; doctors, nurses, and patients; and patients, too, without medical personnel. Patients could not be shut into any one group or *quartier,* but would be transferred about until they felt more at ease. Doctors would work in teams of at least two to three with each patient. Tosquelles felt that a single doctor working with a single patient would not adequately handle oedipal conflicts so often present. Tosquelles thought, too, that patients could be helped by dialogues between doctors. Finally, all activities within the institution should be structured so as to help the patient become aware of his own troubles in order that the cure could begin.†

* *Le Travail thérapeutique à l'hôpital psychiatrique,* p. 53.
† Congrès des médecins aliénistes et neurologues de France et des pays de langue française (Pau, 1953).

For two years Fanon worked closely with Tosquelles, publishing three research papers with the professor directly and three with other of his students. Fanon's medical-reform programs within the hospitals at Blida, Algeria, and Manouba in Tunisia were derived from his education at Saint-Alban. The situations that faced him in North Africa were different from any he had imagined possible: The level of psychiatric care in both institutions might have been described as medieval. Fanon's major energies had to be directed toward bringing his institutions into the twentieth century. His medical career was frustrating in that each time he had renovated his psychiatric service within the institution to the point where he might have begun to experiment with the subtleties of "communal therapy," he was forced, for political reasons, to leave. Fanon always had an underlying urge to move out of politics and back to his first interest: research in new methods of psychotherapy, but he felt the revolution had to succeed to ensure a proper environment for further advances within his own field; it was an unavoidable interruption in what he considered his real work.

There were always interruptions of one kind or another: In the spring of 1953, Fanon had to break off research with Tosquelles in order to review for *Le Médicat des hôpitaux psychiatriques,* the marathon examination preventing so many doctors from becoming psychiatrists in France. In 1953 there were some 150 candidates taking the exam; less than a third passed. Before taking the oral part of the *Médicat,* one had to have completed successfully forty-eight hours of written tests in pathology, neurology, forensic medicine, and other fields—submitted in carbon copies to two separate examiners who would meet after ten days or so to compare the results of their corrections. On July 13, 1953, Joby Fanon sat with

Josie in a reception room outside an examination theater
in the Paris Faculté de Médecine; Frantz Fanon was inside
arguing with certain professors less convinced than he of
the necessity of restructuring psychiatric care within the
nation. As the oral exam dragged on into the early evening, the celebrations of Bastille Day became more audi-
ble: Joby remarked to Josie that he was sure that there
were louder fireworks within the theater. Finally, Fanon
was expected to examine several specially selected patients before seven formally robed physicians; he was
then given a half hour to compose his notes and to read
his diagnoses before the doctors and whoever else cared
to attend the last session of the *Médicat*—an examination
so long and so exacting that success meant assurance of
a position as *chef de service* in a major psychiatric institution
within France.

As a youth, Lenin was entranced with revolution. At
sixteen, he was a revolutionary; by twenty-five, he had a
program for revolution; at forty, he had a revolution. His
party became his life; he was nourished himself by socialist ideology. Frantz Fanon was quite the opposite. At sixteen he was unsure how to feel about the racist French
troops occupying his homeland; by twenty, he was
fighting their war for them. His life, until well after 1954,
was psychiatry, his energies more and more devoted to
medical-reform programs. But by the time that he had
received the title "Psychiatrist," he wanted to get away
from Western racism; he had been indoctrinated with the
concept of *négritude* so important to Césaire and to the
other writers grouped around the Paris publishing house
Présence Africaine. Fanon was offered the directorship of a
Martinican hospital: Although he would have loved to return to the island, there were no facilities there for psy-

chiatric care or research. He then wrote to Léopold Seng-hor, President of Senegal and a writer central to the *Présence Africaine* school, to ask if it would be possible to practice medicine in his country. The letter went unanswered. It was a conflicting situation—wanting to work outside of the West, but still some place where he could be a psychiatrist with a staff and equipment for electro-shock treatment, insulin therapy, and extensive *ergothérapie.* Determined to leave France, Fanon accepted a temporary position as *chef de service* in the psychiatric hospital of Pontorson.

This town, on the Atlantic coast of France, lives off the huge tide of tourists washing in and out of the Abbey of Mont Saint Michel. The hospital, and everything around it, is built out of gray stone almost the shade of the sky above and the tidal marshes dominating the landscape for miles around. The hospital, at least, has rich green lawns and rigidly beautiful formal gardens generously watered by almost daily rains. There are 880 beds and some abnormally depressed doctors. Traveling to Pontorson in 1969, there was still one important question on my mind: the matter of timing. Exactly when did Frantz Fanon become a revolutionary? Until his work at Pontorson, Fanon appeared to be totally immersed in his profession; his political activism fell off after the university years. Did he go to Algeria, as Josie Fanon maintains, because of increasing political tensions there? Or was he radicalized by mounting revolutionary pressures well after his arrival? It seemed hard to imagine Fanon giving up a post in metropolitan France for another institution in overseas France for other than political motivations. But so many of Fanon's Algerian friends, and even his older Martinican acquaintances, claimed that he was in no way a revolutionary when he arrived at Blida, Algeria.

I asked a young psychiatrist, a *chef de service* at Pontorson, why a doctor would give up a position such as his to work in Blida. The psychiatrist looked at me, glanced up at the gray sky, and said, "Listen."

I did. There was absolute silence. That was his point. This doctor himself couldn't wait to get out of this part of Normandy, which he claimed was the most saddening area in the world. He said that any doctor would have jumped at the chance to move to Blida, just outside the large city of Algiers. It was beautiful there, and North African hospitals, at the time, had surpluses of money for research. It would be a step upward in anyone's career. The *chef de service* kept a copy of the *Bulletin Officiel* close by his desk. By law, all of the vacancies for higher positions in French hospitals have to be listed in the government publication. About a month after the trip northward to Pontorson, Fanon read of the opening for a *chef de service* in Algeria; he beat a hasty retreat from the mournful tidal marshes of upper Normandy. It was a compromise: part of the Third World, but not Black Africa or the Antilles.

IV
Blida

One arrives at Blida through the port or airport of Algiers, a city with taller buildings than Paris, some reaching eleven and twelve stories. All are of stucco, cement, or stone painted a gleaming white. From the harbor, on a clear day, Algiers is dazzling, too bright to stare at. Pedestrians within the city are protected from the sun by arcades, the upper stories of the buildings jutting out over the sidewalks. Or else there are carefully trimmed, thick rows of trees serving the same purpose. The least functional aspect of the city is its transportation: Streets are blocked from higher streets by cliffs and buttressing.

One has to walk several long blocks to find a way upward, and then it is often a treacherously steep staircase. Higher up though, a breeze from the Mediterranean helps dry the perspiration; the same air carries the scent of continually flowering trees and bushes throughout the city.

The large modern buildings, the arcades, the breezes and flowers were for the Europeans; the Moslems lived in the darker, closer Casbah, or more likely farther out, away from the cooling sea, in the suburbs filled with huge conglomerations of shanty towns, *bidonvilles,* without running water or electricity. These were the Moslems who had come from the scorched and unfertile areas of the countryside where starvation was still a grave problem. If they were lucky, they would travel to the center of Algiers to work: to repaint the white apartment houses, clean the streets, haul cargo, tend the little parks, sweep up cigarette butts in the huge gambling casino of the elegant Aletti Hotel. Algerian segregation, as in Martinique, was a matter of economics; less than five per cent of the Moslem population had the money to mix freely with the European settlers.

As early as November, 1953, when Fanon arrived in Algiers to present his credentials to the Division of Public Health in the Government General Building, a neo-fascist style of palace sprawling over the city's highest cliff, the French police had begun to enforce a more rigorous political segregation there. After the Second World War, there had been a steady string of incidents of Moslem terrorism against the French administration and settlers. By 1953 the police had isolated the Casbah from the European city with barbed wire, chain-link fences, and police check points. Still, Algiers was perfect terrain for urban guerrilla warfare. There were many narrow, twisting streets outside of the Casbah where a man on a bicycle or motorcycle could escape police. There were masses of Moslem workers everywhere—especially in the richest European quarters—so that a terrorist could always melt into the crowd. Arabic women, in great flowing white robes and veils, could easily hide weapons and bombs; men could pass as women. The French and Algerian newspapers tended to play down North African terrorism; the only way to know of the political tensions there was to work in the territory.

It is a thirty-mile trip southwestward to Blida. One climbs a long series of hills above Algiers to reach the lush farmland with vineyards, fruit trees, and wheat stretching toward this pretty town of sixty thousand persons and white houses with orange-tile roofs. Blida is covered with purple, heavily scented bougainvillaea flowers, a variety of vine that attaches itself to every kind of structure imaginable. In the center of town there is an elegant version of the Savanne in Fort-de-France surrounded by impressively large banks and transportation companies, another indication of the true wealth of the Algerian territory. The hospital is some three miles outside of Blida; it is a self-contained unit stretching over acres of land but isolated amidst even larger wheat fields. Built as a showpiece of French colonialism, the institution's high stone walls surround a hundred separate buildings, landscaped walks, shade trees, varied gardens, a huge cafeteria, staff housing, a rambling administrative center, and wards. The bluish Atlas Mountains, separating this fertile Tell region from the Sahara, tower in the distance above the stone walls. The Fanons' house could best be described as solid—also attractive, roomy, and cool. It had characteristic thick stone walls covered with white stucco and beautifully tiled floors. The five rooms downstairs and bedrooms above were furnished with the

heavy, dark, intricately carved wooden furniture produced in Algeria's Kabyle regions. The hospital provided
every comfort for its staff—at least for the *chefs de service*
and administrators. The nurses and interns, bearing the
brunt of work there, had decrepit and crowded living conditions with very low salaries.

But after a day with the patients in *their* living quarters,
all of the staff could return home with the feeling that they
lived in luxury by comparison. When Fanon arrived at
Blida there were six medical doctors in charge of two
thousand patients. Slightly more than half were European, the rest *indigènes* (natives), in the official language of
the colonial epoch. The two groups were kept separate,
the settlers receiving favored treatment—that is, seeing a
psychiatrist once every ten days or so providing their
behavior had not been violent. The hospital was finally
beginning to use sedatives for the more troublesome patients but strait jackets and chains were still more common. Blida had no facilities for work therapy; all of the
services were "closed" (the patients not allowed to leave
their dormitories and exercise yards). The gardens and
walks outside were for the staff's benefit. Electric shock-
therapy equipment had just arrived at the institution, but
not all of the doctors knew how to use it.

Certain of the six *chefs de service* were appalled at the
institution's inadequacies but were afraid of attacking the
overgrown administration. M. Kriff, the debonair director
of the Blida complex, was never around; he felt compelled
to represent the staff at as many social gatherings as possible in town and in Algiers. In the end, the nurses were
responsible for all aspects of the patients' care; they were
often brutal simply because they lacked the proper training. The doctors and interns neglected the nurses as well
as the patients.

On his first tour of inspection of a ward in his service, Fanon came upon a nurse attending sixty-nine inmates, each strait-jacketed and chained to a bed. He told the male nurse to release every one of the patients. His subordinate looked back at him without understanding. Fanon ejaculated the order again in a more furious tone of voice. As the nurse began to unchain the inmates, other nurses in the pavilion collected about the doorway where they had heard the new doctor raving. Fanon, who had been introduced to them all earlier in the day at a formal reception arranged by M. Kriff, looked toward them and inquired why they were neglecting their own duties. The nurses withdrew slightly but continued to stare at the doctor's unusual performance. He ignored them.

Fanon went to the first patient who had been relieved of his strait jacket. The man continued to lie in bed as though he were still bound there. The doctor introduced himself and explained that he would be available at all times for consultation. He assured him that there would be no strait jackets or chains in the future. Meanwhile the nurse was continuing down the row of beds and freeing patients. Not one stirred. Not one got out of bed. They all stared at the doctor as he continued to talk to each of them. The nurses outside the doorway stood in shocked silence. They feared the new *chef* more than admired him; but he had a kind of self-confidence that could not but impress them.*

In Fanon's service, the distinction between "native" and European was prohibited. On the other hand, the

---

*The descriptions of Fanon's entrance into the institution are from nurses who were there at the time, and still seem to remember every detail of the doctor's behavior.

doctor planned a new kind of segregation based on the patient's aggressiveness.* There would be open wards for those patients who presented no threat of bodily injury to themselves or others; they would be free to enter and leave their wards as they pleased. The hospital grounds, in other times reserved for the staff, would be their domain. There would be varying degrees of segregation in the closed wards too: Most of the patients would be allowed outside of their ward during periods of supervised activities. Each sector of the hospital, under Fanon's supervision, would be divided into small groups of patients living and working together as Tosquelles had provided for at Saint-Alban. The aim of the nurses would be to "graduate" patients through the varying sectors of the closed ward, into the open wards, and out of the hospital. They would always search to locate the patients within compatible groups. There was still a shortage of the new tranquilizing drugs in Algeria, but strait jackets were used only on rare occasions in Fanon's wards.

An American today would consider these reforms minimal; but in North Africa before the Algerian revolution, they were extraordinary. Segregation of the European *colon* from the Moslem masses had been a standard feature of all social life for a century. Mental hospitals were still regarded as places where one stored burdensome relatives till they died. In November, 1953, a twenty-eight-year-old black Martinican came upon the scene to announce directly, and indirectly, that the five other European doctors, the administration, and the interns were either ignorant or negligent. Everything would have to be changed. The staff would have to familiarize itself

---

*Today this kind of classification of mental illness is regarded as obsolete; Fanon, by 1960, was revising his ideas in this area too.

with the work of Tosquelles at Saint-Alban. That was the way of the future.

Fanon didn't think it was necessary to gain backing for his projects; their propriety seemed self-evident. The hospital's director, M. Kriff, never caught up with the new *chef de service,* and was too confused to be angry. He was a bit worried about Blida society's reactions to the Moslem-European integration within Fanon's service, but there were more pressing problems. . . . Fanon, it seems, had already organized a hospital soccer team, requisitioned equipment, and set up a schedule of matches with local teams around Blida. It was during the second, or perhaps the third match that an administrative official found that a good number of Fanon's patients, as well as the *chef,* were missing from the institution. Kriff was in a panic, and telephoned the *préfet's* office to report the "possibility" of what might best be described as a jail break. Kriff must have looked rather silly that afternoon when Fanon's bus returned with the hospital's victorious team, which the director didn't know existed.

Fanon accentuated older cleavages within the medical staff. Dr. Lacaton, a younger *chef de service,* had felt the necessity for reform before Fanon's arrival, but he needed a push to redo his own service. He and Fanon could give a more modern kind of care to almost seven hundred patients between them; the other four *chefs* resisted any kind of change. The subordinates, nurses and interns, in services other than Lacaton's and Fanon's, felt ashamed to be part of the *ancien régime.* They began to make small changes in all the pavilions of the hospital when the doctors were not around. The reactionary staff was not interested enough in the details of its services to react against the changes. Still, there was resentment: Behind his back certain of the European staff members referred to Fanon as the "Arab Doctor," their version of "Nigger Doctor."

A number of the male nurses surrounding Fanon in 1954 remember his attitude as belligerent, oversensitive, and angry. But the anger was sublimated into the most useful sorts of criticisms. Fanon, these nurses explained, knew that he could never be accepted into the colonial society dominating both the hospital and all of Algeria; nor did he want to be; but he would make no compromises with this society. Another segment of the staff members who worked under Fanon describe him as being more detached and scientific. They claim that he had extraordinary self-confidence, the result of total dedication to his work. The former associates of Fanon offer a more plausible argument—especially when they compare him with Dr. Lacaton, who was just as well trained as Fanon but unable to begin serious hospital reforms before the other's arrival. Lacaton, slightly older than Fanon, came to North Africa to make his career there; he was just as radical as Fanon, but not angry enough to ignore the feelings of his colleagues and superiors. Recognizing Fanon's driving force as hostility cannot in any way diminish the nature of his accomplishments at Blida. As one nurse said, "He brought us into the twentieth century." And it was nurses and interns together who were behind the campaign to change the name of the institution to the "Hôpital Psychiatrique Frantz Fanon" after 1962.

From the outset, the majority of doctors and administrators within the hospital would see no more of Fanon than was absolutely necessary during the day's work. The institution was a self-contained unit outside of Blida and almost two hours away from Algiers; one had to construct a social life within the hospital or have none at all. Fanon avoided this problem somewhat by working incredible hours six or seven days a week. He had cut his sleeping

time down to four hours a night; he could enter the three
buildings of his service at all hours to check on developments; it was not unusual to find him in his office at four
in the morning. When he was off from work, Fanon could
rely on the company of only one or two medical doctors,
and several interns; his real friends were the Moslem
nurses within his service. He had only a few European
allies in the hospital: Dr. Lacaton and three interns, Sanchez, Geronomi and Azoulay. The nurses, as a group,
were extremely intelligent and sensitive human beings,
many of whom would have been doctors were it not for
the segregation and exploitation by colonial rule in North
Africa. Fanon, engrossed in new projects for therapy,
suffered less from not having a wide circle of friends than
did his wife Josie. She was a nervous and occasionally
dogmatic person very conscious of her position as wife to
a black Martinican not well received by the ruling powers
in the hospital world. She would often see insults to her
husband when there were none intended; and she tended
to stay out of hospital life. Even though the isolation of the
pretty, but empty house might have been depressing, her
avenues of escape were limited. A woman has difficulties
being independent in Algeria: Unescorted females
were never welcomed in Moslem eating or drinking
places; a woman without a robe or veil had to stay
pretty much within colonialist circles, or else remain
at home.

Occasionally, the Fanons were able to import company:
After 1955, Manville came to Algiers on business trips.
He was one of the few French attorneys who had the confidence of the Algerian nationalists, and who was willing to
defend those accused of anti-French terrorism.* Fanon

---

*Later Manville's office in Paris was bombed by right-wing terrorists,
but he escaped injury.

and Manville had the same kind of lighthearted friendship
as always, and, as before, the doctor tended to become
carried away with his "jokes." By 1955 the police had set
up a major check point on the highway running from
Algiers to Blida on a long, banked curve where the cars
and trucks were forced to slow up before they were ordered to stop. Fanon had been chatting about the increasing revolutionary tensions, and perhaps he didn't think
Manville fully appreciated the new situation. As he went
into the curve he began to speed up; Manville started to
stutter about stopping. Fanon raced past the first soldiers
with machine guns, and just as they were swinging them
around on the vehicle headed toward the second emplace-
ment of soldiers, he locked the brakes and skidded to a
stop. A rifle barrel was jammed into the front window as
a soldier snarled, "Ten more meters and you would have
been dead." They were cleared, and began to drive on;
Manville conceded that Fanon had made his point. Another time, the two of them were stopped outside of Blida.
Manville had left his wallet at the hospital. The police
wouldn't let him continue on until he established his identity, and had him start walking back toward Blida at gun
point. Manville asked Fanon what would happen and received the unemotional response, "They'll probably kill
you. They'll say you tried to escape." With that Fanon
hopped into his car to go back to the hospital to get
Manville's identity cards.

The French occupied Algiers in the 1830s to control
piracy along that stretch of the southern Mediterranean
coast. During the next decade the Europeans moved inland to the rich farming areas in order to re-enforce
French claims to a new African colony. Alexis de Tocqueville, traveling through North Africa in the 1840s, noted

some of the worse features of his country's colonization
policy:

> Even in the environs of Algiers, fertile land has been
> taken from Arabs and given to Europeans who are
> not able, or do not wish, to cultivate it themselves,
> and who have rented it back to the same natives—now
> tenant farmers on land that was their fathers'. Else-
> where tribes or parts of tribes that have not been
> hostile to us, even more, that have fought with us and
> sometimes without us have been expelled from their
> land. We have made agreements with them that have
> not been kept, we have promised indemnities that
> have not been paid—allowing our honor to suffer
> more than the interests of the natives.*

The French themselves weren't particularly anxious to
cross the Mediterranean to the new territory; so the
French government peopled it with poorer refugees from
other parts of southern Europe. In 1954 there were nine
million Moslems in Algeria and a million French citizens,
but less than half of these were of French stock. There
were more than 300,000 Europeans of Spanish descent in
the countryside around Oran. Oran and Bône had about
100,000 settlers of Italian and Maltese background. There
were also 140,000 Jews in Algeria who had been made
French citizens by the Cremieux decrees in 1870. And
there was a large bloc of Corsican settlers.

In the settlers' lingo, the Moslems remained *melons*
("simps"), or *ratons* ("coons"); "They weigh in the
scales," a European mayor, Raymond Laquierre, said, "as
feathers against gold."† Before the Second World War

---

*"Rapport fait par M. de Tocqueville à la Chambre des deputés,"
Journal Officiel (May 24, 1847).
†Quoted from J. Kraft's excellent article, "Settler Politics in Algeria,"
Foreign Affairs (July, 1961).

the vast majority of Moslems were denied any kind of suffrage at all; afterward they voted in an electoral college separate but unequal to the Europeans; all was arranged to give the one-million minority of French citizens absolute power within the territory. In 1954, 90 per cent of the Europeans were engaged in non-agricultural pursuits, mostly petit bourgeois urban occupations. Still, there were 5,000 *colons* owning one-third of all the best land in Algeria. The settlers had a long tradition of lining up with the extreme right-wing political parties in France. In the 1890s Algeria was a center of anti-Dreyfusard movements; after the First World War Jacques Doriot established his French Fascist Party from Algiers; Pétain's rightist regime was welcomed in all of Algeria.

At the same time, the nine million Moslems had at least a 43 per cent unemployment rate. The Moslem's average yearly income in 1954 was about forty dollars. In Algeria there was one doctor for every 5,005 persons, one dentist for every 19,434. Ninety per cent of the Moslems were illiterate. There were more than half a million fellahs, Moslem farmers trying to eke out a living on small plots of about twenty acres: One-fifth of them survived on farms of less than three acres. There were sixty thousand sharecroppers.

Although the *Front de Libération Nationale* announced November, 1954, as the beginning of the struggle for independence, one could just as well choose earlier dates on which terrorists struck against the French domination of the territory. By the end of the Second World War an increasing nationalist fervor grew out of the extreme poverty of the masses. In the city of Sétif, in 1945, nationalists organized a parade around the theme of Algerian independence. French police units smashed the demonstration by firing into the ranks of the thousands parading.

French settlers, nervous and furious at the show of separatist feelings, also began firing into the parade. It was quickly decided to liquidate the entire Moslem organization that had planned the demonstration—to make an example for the rest of the territory. The settlers had what they jokingly referred to as an "Open Season on Arabs," shooting any non-European who happened to be on the streets at the wrong time. By the end of the month some forty thousand Moslems and Berbers were dead in and around Sétif. This bloody repression fertilized the strong roots of decolonization.

The French empire was not functioning well in other parts of the world either. After the Second World War there was open warfare against the Europeans in Indochina; and Paris had to contend with increasing nationalist pressures in Tunisia and Morocco. Algerians in the metropolitan territory, as well as in North Africa, were organized into their own *Mouvement pour le Triomphe des Libertés Démocratiques,* which endorsed "militant" action for independence but hesitated about calling for terrorism. In 1947, though, Ait Ahmed set up the smaller *Organisation Spéciale,* which began collecting money and arms for an immediate war against the French. In 1949, Ahmed Ben Bella, who had been decorated four times by the French forces during the Second World War, took over the O. S.'s campaign of terrorism against the administration within the Algerian territory. By 1954 the O. S. had expanded into the *Comité Révolutionnaire d'Unité d'Action* uniting many nationalist leaders from older organizations that had, in the past, shunned violence. They now agreed that war was the only possible path toward independence. The *Front de Libération Nationale* became an important force only after the Soummam Valley meeting of 1956, but the F.L.N. accepted C.R.U.A.'s earlier actions, the terrorism after November, 1954, as the beginning of the campaign for independence.

Two hundred nationalist leaders came together in the rugged Soummam Valley in August, 1956, to lend some order to the anti-French campaigns of the previous years. A thirty-four member National Council would henceforth set the wider guidelines for the revolution and direct the administration of the six wilayas (revolutionary zones) of Algeria. The F.L.N. would be the mass political party leading the new nation toward socialism. The *Armée de Libération Nationale,* or A.L.N., was subordinate to the civilian political rule of the party and the Council. Soummam established the infrastructure of a new nation that had the automatic allegiance of the masses by virtue of a century of European misrule.

V
The Algerian Front

In the cold of Europe [Céline wrote in *Journey to the End of the Night*], under the prudish northern fogs, except when slaughter is afoot, you only glimpse the crawling cruelty of your fellow men. But their rottenness rises to the surface as soon as they are tickled by the hideous fevers of the tropics. It's then that the wild unbuttoning process begins, and degradation triumphs, taking hold of us entirely. A biological confession of weakness. As soon as work and the cold restrain us no longer, as soon as their stranglehold is loosened you catch sight in the white race of what you see on a pretty beach when the tide goes out:

reality, heavy-smelling pools of slime, the crabs, the carcasses and scum.*

Albert Camus, in *The Stranger,* effectively described the appalling strength of the Algerian sunlight. But Camus was writing about the coastland, where the breezes mitigate the heat. The town of Blida lies inland, where the air is much stiller and where the sun only gives way to a peculiar kind of hot rainstorm. In the summer of 1956, when Fanon was there, slaughter was afoot: A searing war had stripped away the last vestiges of humanity from the settlers, the French army, and the administration. For professional reasons as well as politics, tensions within the hospital were unbearable: The resentment against Fanon's clique, which would voice no opposition to the revolution, had escalated to dangerous heights. First the police arrested a number of the doctor's male nurses; then the brunt of the fury fell upon Fanon's admirer, Dr. Lacaton. All it took was a few words to the Blida officials: Soon the police entered the hospital grounds to arrest Lacaton on the suspicion of collaborating with the nationalist forces. Back in town, the doctor was subjected to the standard methods of interrogation for the period. First, direct, simple questions: "Do you work for the F.L.N.?" "Who is your superior?" "Who works with you?" "If you're not part of the F.L.N., is there anyone else in the hospital whom you suspect of having anti-French feelings?" Then, when there were no satisfactory answers, a little pushing around. The police would take turns punching the doctor. Quite often, when dealing with a European, the officials were more brutal than with a Moslem. It was assumed that the European was a traitor to his own

---

*Louis-Ferdinand Céline, *Journey to the End of the Night,* trans. by J.P. Marks, (New York: New Directions, 1960), p. 110.

"race." If beatings produced no satisfactory results, the police would turn to more sophisticated methods of inter-rogation. They would force-feed water down the throat; give enemas of soapy water; submerge a victim in a bath-tub until he was just about to suffocate. The larger police stations had special electrical shock equipment that was used on the genital area. In the end, it didn't particularly matter if the victim had information or not; those in charge came to consider the torture a routine activity. In Lacaton's case, after the torture, the police decided that he was not directly involved in F.L.N. activity. But it was also clear that he was not totally dedicated to the war against Moslem separatism. It was decided to release him in the manner reserved for such ambiguous personalities. The black police van drove the doctor into the Algerian countryside to a large pig farm owned by a European settler who enjoyed co-operating with the government in every possible manner. Half unconscious from his treat-ment at the police station, Lacaton was thrown into a pigsty. Had he been more seriously injured during the earlier questioning, he would never have escaped from the pigs alive. But Lacaton survived, and after regaining a semblance of health, packed up and left the handsome, modern, well-equipped French psychiatric hospital at Blida.

The same kind of treatment awaited Fanon each day that he remained. There can be no doubt that he was an extremely brave man. Nor did Fanon slacken his activities in support of the revolution. By a process of natural politi-cal and social evolution, his own service in the hospital came to be staffed by the interns and nurses who were already deeply involved in the war effort against the French. At certain times the hospital ambulance would bring in nationalist soldiers from the countryside; Fanon or a nurse would treat their wounds; then the ambulance would take the men back to their original position. Some of the more seriously wounded remained in Fanon's wards as "psychiatric cases"—attempted suicides and such. There were those working within the hospital administration who could always provide a little extra room, a few extra beds, in Fanon's pavilions for nationalist soldiers. The police continued to arrest individual nurses as they had Dr. Lacaton but the authorities never realized the extent of the nationalist organization within the hospital. But perhaps "organization" is the wrong word: There were never any political meetings and secrecy was always of uppermost importance. Medical personnel knew only about their own duties within the revolution—they did not want to know more. Nor did they discuss this kind of thing with their families or friends. If tortured by the police, one should not be *able* to say too much. The nurses in Fanon's service were better informed about his revolutionary life than was Fanon's wife; but this is only because they were part of this life, with their own specific duties to perform within it.

When Dr. Lacaton was questioned by the police, he could have guessed that Fanon was working for the F.L.N. But he did not know this for sure; he was well-informed only about the political activities within his own service. This was as much as he ever wanted to know. Anyone in a situation like this who attempted to gain a general knowledge of the revolutionary structure within an institution or a specific area of Algeria was suspected of being a counterrevolutionary. Fanon himself became well informed about the Algerian revolution only when this became his assigned task within the revolution's Ministry of Information. Even then, there was mystery: Fanon, along with all of the other revolutionary leaders, operated under continually changing pseudonyms.

It is hard to say why Fanon himself escaped arrest while at Blida. Perhaps it was because he was always considered a foreigner (he was black and from the Americas), and for some reason security officials usually gave foreigners more leeway than they did Algerian Moslems or settlers. The government, one would have to speculate, did not want an international audience for its methods of interrogation. More important, though, Fanon was so open about his feelings that it would have been hard to imagine him simultaneously working for the *Front de Libération Nationale.* To give an instance: There was an air force base close to the hospital, and with each escalation of the warfare the number of planes taking off over the hospital increased. Sometimes, throughout a night, jet bombers would come in and out of the base making a deafening roar over the wards. Fanon, along with the other doctors, knew that the planes were disturbing the patients' sleep and retarding their recovery; but only Fanon dared to complain. In fact, he went to the Chief-of-Staff of the air force in Algeria, then to the Resident Minister's office, to complain about the noise, explain the situation, and request that the patterns of air flights be altered to preserve the restful atmosphere of the institution. For a year or so, the French air force tried to comply with Fanon's request. The hospital people were, on the one hand, impressed with the doctor's "rapport" with higher officials in the territory and, on the other hand, less sure that he was quite as subversive as he sounded. He had presented his views to the army; they had not arrested him but had instead tried to respect his petition.

Fanon was less successful when he returned to the Resident Minister's office to complain about other worsening conditions for practicing psychiatry in Algeria. The theme of this second petition may be found in the "Letter of Resignation" that he sent to the same office a year later:

> If psychiatry is a medical technique which seeks to restore man to a proper contact with his environment it must be stressed that the Arab, always treated as an alien in his own nation, is forced to live in an inhuman condition.
>
> The law in Algeria is in fact a systematic process of dehumanization. . . . The social structure existing in Algeria makes it impossible to restore the human being to his proper place.*

Fanon resented the continual police intrusions into hospital life: the searches there at all hours of the day and night, the coming and going of the familiar black van, gendarmes strutting about the grounds. Much worse, a number of nurses had disappeared after the police had taken them for questioning—victims of official murder. In all instances of Fanon's contact with the police, it was assumed that the Arabs, and Europeans who were friendly with Arabs, were guilty of unspecified crimes. The doctor was able to describe certain of his patients' paranoid behavior as a normal reaction to the existing conditions. Naturally, telling the Resident Minister all of this could not alter the territory's political and social structure, but the doctor did manage to bring about small changes in hospital routine that helped to improve living conditions there. In 1955, because of Fanon, police were no longer permitted to carry loaded guns when they entered the hospital grounds. If possible they were to complete their business in the guardhouse at the gate of the institution. These might seem like small matters, yet they provided a

---

*The "Letter of Resignation" is in Fanon's *Pour la révolution africaine* (Paris: Maspero, 1964), pp. 59 ff.

minimum of insulation for the patients against the terror of a war that had often ruined their lives outside.

Fanon's psychiatric therapy was always intermeshed with the war. His patients were not only the victims of the fighting but also the agents of the oppression. He worked with one European policeman who could not sleep at night because of imaginary screaming. Each evening the officer made his wife close the windows and shutters of their hot Algiers apartment. He tried to stuff his ears with cotton before getting into bed. When he couldn't sleep, he would turn the radio on at full blast to cover the "screaming." This disturbance was the result of the policeman's daily attendance at torture sessions. He told Fanon:

> Nowadays as soon as I hear someone shouting I can tell you exactly at what stage of the questioning we've got to. The chap who's had two blows of the fist and a belt of the baton behind his ear has a certain way of speaking, of shouting. . . . After he's been left two hours strung up by his wrists he has another kind of voice. . . . But above all it's after the electricity that it becomes really too much.*

This law officer was intelligent enough to know that he had to change his job to recover from the affliction, and after he had requested a transfer Fanon continued to give him therapy within his own home on the hospital grounds. (The officer, quite naturally, was afraid of the Moslems whom he had tortured, and could not go into the open ward.) Once, when the officer was awaiting Fanon outside of Fanon's home, he happened upon one of his former victims, now a patient in the hospital. The victim was found, half an hour later, in a hospital washroom trying

---

* *The Wretched of the Earth* (New York: Grove Press, 1968), p. 265.

to commit suicide. Fanon's therapy consisted, for the
most part, of trying to push for the officer's transfer outside of Algeria. At the same time, the doctor was attempting to reassure the Moslem that he had not really seen the
officer, that the police were not allowed on hospital
grounds, that he was extremely fatigued and needed rest,
and so on.

A year earlier Fanon had treated another police officer
who had decided to consult a "nerve specialist" after a
stormy night when he had begun to torture his own wife.
He complained to the doctor:

> Nowadays we have to work like troopers. . . . Those
> gentlemen in the government say there's no war in
> Algeria and that the arm of the law, that's to say the
> police, ought to restore order. But there *is* a war
> going on in Algeria, and when they wake up to it it'll
> be too late. The thing that kills me most is the torture.
> You don't know what that is, do you? Sometimes I
> torture people for ten hours at a stretch. . . .
>
>   You may not realize it, but that's tiring. . . . It's true
> we take turns, but the question is to know when to let
> the next chap have a go. Each one thinks he's going
> to get the information at any minute and takes good
> care not to let the bird go to the next chap after he's
> softened him up nicely. . . . Our problem is as follows:
> Are you able to make this fellow talk? It's a question
> of personal success. You see, you're competing with
> the others. . . .*

The officer scoffed at Fanon's suggestion that he change
his line of work. No, all he wanted was that the doctor
help him get ahead within the police department;
and he wished for a more relaxed life outside of work.

---

* *Ibid.*, p. 268.

Fanon could not continue with the therapy.

These two cases reveal something of Fanon too—how he became a revolutionary. Obviously, he had not been one of the F.L.N.'s *chefs historiques* who had opened the new separatist campaign in November, 1954, but rather an outsider drawn into the conflict by the ferocity of colonial repression. Fanon had always been miles apart from M. Kriff, the director of the hospital, as well as from the European administration that he represented; but entering the nationalist war effort was another matter. The doctor might have been radicalized by numerous evidences of mass Moslem poverty as well as continued conversations with the nurses, but it was French murder and torture that cut the last attachment to the metropolitan civilization. By 1956 Fanon was sure that to take a meaningful stand against fascism in North Africa he had to be part of the *Front de Libération Nationale*.

The notes from the cases of the European police agents, part of the last chapter of *The Wretched of the Earth*, are brief, lacking in detail, and superficial in terms of therapy. None of Fanon's case notes, which are still in the hospital archives today, are of much greater length or depth than those in the last part of his book. It seems that usually the doctor's observations were dictated to nurses; the notes have few direct quotations from the patients themselves. In many instances the case histories were the work of the nurses, with some editing by Fanon. There are reasons for this. With only six doctors for two thousand patients he could not spare the time for detailed notes. His career was dedicated to the masses. His school of "communal therapy" would construct new social environments to aid greater numbers of patients at one time as compared to other schools that concentrated on refining methods of individual therapy.

Not all of Fanon's work at Blida was successful; his most interesting notes come from his great failure there—his attempt to integrate Moslem and European therapy.* Sometime after he completed his basic reforms within the hospital—freeing the patients of burdensome institutional regulations; dividing his pavilions into smaller living and working groups; creating new work therapy facilities; retraining nurses; giving the patients parties, entertainment, their own newspaper and cafés—the doctor noticed that the discharge rate of Europeans was much greater than that of Moslems. Moreover the Moslem men were beginning to try to avoid work therapy sessions; they had little interest in group activities; they didn't care about movies or entertainment. Fanon and his colleagues set up carefully planned meetings with the Moslems to try and ascertain their grievances against the new programs; the most intelligent nurses were to be used as translators. The meetings, and in fact all therapy, were greeted with hostility or indifference. The whole reform program was becoming less and less successful within the Moslem wards. The nurses too were becoming impatient; they wanted the doctor to return to older methods of "punishment"—strait jackets and chains. One of the nurses explained to Fanon, "You're still young and don't understand the Algerians. When you've been working with them for fifteen years like us, you'll understand. . . ." The group meetings, as well as the therapy, became

---

*The outlines of the failure are given in F. Fanon and J. Azoulay, "La Socialthérapie dans un service d'hommes musulmans," *L'Information Psychiatrique*, No. 9 (1954), pp. 349–361—an article extracted from a longer medical thesis done by Azoulay, under Fanon's guidance, *Contribution à l'étude de la socialthérapie dans un service d'aliénés musulmans*, submitted to the Faculté de Médecine, University of Algiers, 1954.

in Fanon's own words, "only an empty ceremony, absurd, and after thinking about the matter we decided to suspend them." The doctor tried smaller meetings, with the nurses, and no Europeans present; they too were a failure.

Fanon, along with Lacaton and Azoulay, a third doctor interested in the reforms, had a meeting with the nurses to discuss the breakdown of the program—not a complete breakdown because, in general, the Europeans had been responding well. It became clear to Fanon that his egalitarian attitude toward the patients was not correct: What he had been doing, in reality, was to impose European solutions on Moslem problems. He had been treating the Algerians as though they were French—carrying into effect the French colonial policy of "assimilation." "But assimilation," Fanon wrote in his case notes, "does not suppose any kind of reciprocity. There is always a culture which has to disappear to the profit of another culture." Fanon and his colleagues had begun their reforms with the assumption that there was no need to understand the Algerian within his own cultural contest, that he could be cured in the context of European society. Everything from the hospital newspaper, through the entertainment and the meetings, was set up in Western style.

Fanon returned to the structuralist approach of his old teacher, Tosquelles; this meant, in effect, trying to recreate the Moslem personality within Moslem society. The doctors began to study certain very basic features of Moslem life: the central importance of religion in social life; the unusual strength of the family unit; the tight groups of families; the dependency of females. Fanon and his colleagues examined a service of 212 Moslem men to find that seventy-six of them were agricultural laborers, thirty-five small farmers, seventy-five urban workers, and twenty-six without any profession. The fact that so much of Algerian life was centered about agriculture gave a clue to the failure of work therapy programs within the hospital; the Moslems were for the most part unable to comprehend the necessity or enjoyment of the craft work and other kinds of indoor labor that were part of the therapy. Several months or years in the hospital were insufficient to obliterate their past attachment to the land.

The reasons for smaller failures in the hospital became clear. The Moslems were not enthusiastic about the new cafés that Fanon had set up because women were permitted into them. Nor would Moslem women enter a café where there were men. Originally, too, Fanon had thought that the five or six educated patients within the services would disseminate the news from the hospital newspaper, *Notre Journal,* throughout the ward; he had not reckoned on the fact that they were not professional storytellers, a highly specialized occupation within a society where the oral tradition was still of uppermost importance.

The doctors assessed their biggest failure as being a matter of language. The use of nurse translators had been totally inadequate. Whereas most of the doctors' ideas had been communicated to the patients, the Moslems' emotions and reactions had not survived translation into French. Meetings and therapy had been frustrating ordeals for the Moslems. Fanon began to requisition the services of one of his nurses for Arabic lessons; by the end of 1956 he could understand most of what patients were telling him.

"Biology, psychology, and sociology," Fanon concluded about the first period in Blida, "were never separated except by the narrowness of our interpretation." He and his colleagues had particularly neglected the sociology of the Algerian society within which they worked. Soon, though, the doctors were setting up work-therapy programs around manual labor outside of the wards; the most successful project involved giving patients their own garden plots and having the hospital buy the produce. Inside the wards, Moslem social life was henceforth centered around religious holidays and festivals. Fanon hired professional storytellers to enter the hospital at periodic intervals. Formal meetings involving patients, doctors, and translators were held to a minimum; Fanon had found that Moslems associated such stiffly structured sessions with past injustices suffered at the hands of the French administration of the territory. The doctors negated an old regulation forbidding Moslem women to wear veils outside of the wards; and Fanon set up another café reserved for women.

Both the failures and the discoveries at Blida might today seem obvious to someone with a bit of training in social psychiatry. Yet we are dealing here with the history of French psychiatry—in a colonial area—almost two decades ago. In that context the doctors' work is more impressive. Fanon's respect for traditional cultural patterns stopped short of their interfering with modern medical techniques. He classified the medicine men, witch doctors, and marabouts operating in the Algerian countryside as agents of Western colonialism helping to keep the territory enslaved in ignorance and weakness. In practice the doctor's tactics against folkloric medicine were more subtle. When a patient made continued demands for a marabout or medicine man, Fanon would try to get this kind of person into the hospital in order to treat some simple physical malady in a ward. After giving the visitor a certain amount of time to cure the illness, Fanon would give him his fee and then himself take over the case. Usually, with the aid of medications, he could quickly outdo the country doctor. He would use one example like this within an entire ward to try and discredit the traditional kind of medicine.

Fanon's new newspaper in the hospital, *Notre Journal*, never worked out the way he had envisaged it would. The Moslems couldn't read, nor did the European patients care much about writing for it; the paper was most successful in providing a new kind of work therapy to those who printed it. Reading through several years of the back issues re-enforces the concept of Fanon, quite often alone, continuing to work for a better hospital amidst the apathy and hostility of most of his peers, the European doctors. Each weekly issue had an editorial by Fanon; the rest of the paper was the work of the nurses; once in a great while there was an article by a patient. The only other doctor who ever contributed to *Notre Journal* was Lacaton. Fanon used the paper to defend his own reforms within the institution and as part of the new training program for nurses. Weekly, the doctor would describe details of new plans for extended work therapy as well as remind the staff of the benefits that had accrued from older projects. Each ward had its own section within the paper in which nurses would speak of the patients' gardens, the woodwork completed, plans for religious celebrations, the fabrics being woven in the women's workshops, and so on. *Notre Journal* continued to urge all of the staff and patients to think of new ways to make daily life within the institution more interesting and pleasant. Fanon's column always chided the nurses who acted as "referees in soccer games" or who tended to take on the role of the patients' guardians. The nurses' real task was to make the hospital into a viable society by encouraging increased patient and staff participation in all aspects of institutional life.

It is difficult to remember that the doctor was giving this advice amidst a bloody war and revolution. Fanon's whole life at this point might be described as impossible: At night he would be removing shrapnel from a nationalist soldier's leg; the next day he would be just as conscientious about organizing the patients' first excursions outside of the hospital to the beach. In the early morning, the doctor would discharge an F.L.N. recruit who had been resting from shell shock; at noon he would take a tour of the spring gardens and inspect the newest completed fabrics from the female patients' looms. During lunch hour the same day the ambulance would bring in the nationalists' political commissar for the Blida region almost dead from an encounter with the French police; in the afternoon Fanon would be in the office of the hospital's administrative director going over plans for increased religious facilities within the institution. Here and there, during the day, he would use ten or fifteen minutes to write—a column for *Notre Journal* or an article for a nationalist publication; he was not, at this period, working on a book.

By 1956 he had moved into the nationalist camp; there was no longer any room for political neutrality in Algeria. The French were conducting the war with a totalitarian brutality: Liberals and centrists were considered as part of the enemy; the opposition was not even allowed lawyers. Fanon's friend in Paris, Manville, received a letter:

You are aware, no doubt, of the imprisonment of all of the Algerian lawyers that we had chosen for our defense.

Our case comes up on appeal on the 18th of March

in 1957. I have, therefore, the need of your counsel
as quickly as possible. . . .*

It was one of many frenzied appeals for help from all
levels of Algerian society. The French, in this period, were
experimenting with new methods of counter-insurgency
warfare including relocation of massive numbers of the
Moslem population. In rural areas peasants were taken off
their own land and herded into barbed-wire-enclosed barracks and yards guarded by French soldiers; any Moslems
caught outside of the camps could be shot as rebels. In the
cities, suspected liberals were removed from their jobs
and put in Assigned Residence. These Algerians were at
least well educated enough to articulate their outrage: 140
of the victims of this kind of oppression sent a petition to
the Resident Minister from their "residence camp" at
Lodi:

> "Assigned Residence," "Relocation Center"—very
> vague expressions, as you must know—because we
> are obliged to live in buildings guarded by armed
> soldiers, caged in with barbed wire; our mail is cen-
> sored—including letters from lawyers, our doctors,
> and our business associates. . . .
> This is, Monsieur le Ministre, a description of how
> we live:
> —140 of us in three rooms with an average of ten
> cubic yards of air space for each one.
> —beds attached to the floor without the possibility
> of moving them.
> —no permission to leave the rooms to walk in the
> single outdoor courtyard of the camp.†

*The complete letter in P. Kessel and G. Pirelli, *Le Peuple algérien et la
guerre: lettres et témoignages, 1954–1962* (Paris: Maspero, 1962), p. 121.
†*Ibid.*, pp. 76 ff.

Petitions such as this, when they did manage to reach the government, were rarely answered. Living conditions all over Algeria had become so desperate that refugees risked their lives to stream over the carefully guarded borders of Tunisia and Morocco. The neighboring nations tried to provide for the Algerians as best as they could, but two American professors visiting one camp of refugees in Tunisia wrote:

> Hundreds of them—and these are the fortunate ones who have been taken out of the hell that is Algeria . . . remain in agglomerate misery, starving slowly, with rickety, spindly legs, unhealthy swollen bellies. . . . Some were blind or else half-blind from trachoma. Tuberculosis was prevalent among them. . . . There were children who still wore bandages over war wounds. There were permanently crippled children, and there were children who were mad because of what they had seen.*

Much of Fanon's regular work in the hospital was with the victims of the war, the Moslems who were lucky enough to be sent to the institution after torture as well as a number of Europeans actually in charge of the torture. One of the cases that he recalled as being particularly interesting involved a patient who arrived with two fractures of the jaw from police beatings.† After two weeks of intravenous injections and rest, he could begin to talk. He was one of the "assimilated" Moslems: As a youth he had been one of the principal leaders of the Moslem Scout Movement, and afterward a highly trained specialist in multicopying machines. He had European features and

---

*R. and J. Brace, *Algerian Voices* (Princeton: D. Van Nostrand, 1965), pp. 89, 90.
†The outlines of the case are to be found in *The Wretched of the Earth*, pp. 274 ff.

could live in settler society. Yet after 1954 he felt increasingly uneasy until a year later he began to isolate himself even from his family; he felt that other Moslems considered him a "traitor" to the nationalist movement. He heard voices calling him a coward:

> As a contrast to this, beside him Algerian men and women were arrested, maltreated, insulted, and searched. Paradoxically, he had no papers on him. This uncalled-for consideration toward him on the part of the enemy patrols confirmed his delusion that "everybody knew he was with the French. Even the French soldiers had orders; they left him alone."*

One day when he was walking past the headquarters of the French General Staff, he found himself attacking a guard and shouting, "I am Algerian." He was of course taken to prison and interrogated under the usual procedures; but it was evident that he was insane. French judicial authorities turned the prisoner over to the Blida hospital for "legal advice"; Fanon became his doctor because of his earlier specialization in forensic medicine.† Once the story was told, the patient began to understand the social and political implications of his own troubles. The cure was underway. . . .

Fanon himself had been a successful, assimilated Frenchman—now, in a rational state of mind, he was stating, through his actions, that he was Algerian. He always tended to become totally engaged—whether fighting in the Second World War or in psychiatric reform afterward.

Ibid., pp. 274, 275.
†Fanon wrote a theoretical paper on legal guilt within the North African Moslem environment: *"Conduites d'aveu en Afrique du Nord"* for the Congrès des médecins aliénistes et neurologues de France et des pays de langue française (Nice, September 5–11, 1955).

He was a Nietzschean figure hating inaction above all. He had suffered, in indirect ways, from European racism, through his people in Martinique and through the Moslems in Algeria. He had never forgotten the children fighting over garbage in North Africa during his army days. The sojourn at Blida allowed, or even forced, Fanon to act on the principles in which he had always believed. Joining the nationalists was not as difficult as it might sound; they were everywhere and appreciated help from any quarter. Fanon's first liaisons with the nationalists were of a medical nature; then his writing brought him deeper into the center of the F.L.N. camp.

Fanon established his own revolutionary potential in the conclusion to his first book, where he finally announced that for the blacks working in the fields of the Martinican sugar plantations there was only one solution —to fight. He increased his reputation as an intelligent social commentator, outside of his psychiatric work, in the review *L'Esprit* and writing for *Conscience Maghrebine.* * Pierre Chaulet, an unusual figure within the nationalist movement, was working for this last publication too, and met Fanon in 1955. This blond-haired, youthful-looking son of a European settler was finishing his own medical studies in Algiers when he was sent to Blida to set up a local unit of *Les Amitiés Algériennes,* supposedly a charitable organization, but one which was actually used by the F.L.N. to channel funds toward the needy families of nationalist warriors. Chaulet knew exactly what he was doing; he had been working with the nationalists since the beginning of the revolution; and he got on well with Fanon from their first meeting. One evening, after a relax-

---

*"Antillais et Africains," *L'Esprit* (February, 1955); "Réflexions sur la ethnopsychiatrie," *Conscience Maghrebine*, No. 3 (1955).

ing dinner with the Fanons at the hospital, and after listening to some jazz records, Chaulet began to describe the underground F.L.N. publications for which he worked. Somewhat later, Fanon himself began to contribute to the same periodicals. The two remained friends throughout the revolution, working together for the F.L.N. newspaper as well as in various nationalist health centers throughout Tunisia.

Through his work, Fanon continued to rise in the revolutionary hierarchy. After meeting Chaulet, he was able to give medical aid to the top F.L.N. administrator in the Algiers area. Si Saddek was actually hidden in the doctor's own house while he recovered, during a week of heavy sedation, from a severe attack of nervous exhaustion. Certain of Fanon's subordinates maintain that during 1956 the F.L.N. also was hiding arms and munitions in the doctor's pavilions, but this is hard to substantiate.

Occasionally, the nurses at Blida who have the deepest respect for Fanon will admit that they never could enjoy working for him. Increasing tensions of war served to make him a pure terror. Fanon expected the same performance from his subordinates that he required from himself—not a reasonable demand. The nurses' school, one of his most important medical projects, could become a hellish ordeal for the students within it. Each nurse had to take a periodic board examination run by other nurses and interns who were more advanced in their training. Fanon always encouraged rigorous questioning. Making a fool of the student being questioned or ridiculing an unintelligent question posed by another nurse were established methods of demonstrating superior achievement. During an examination Fanon would suddenly become angry. His eyes would flash, his body tense, his face become drawn out. He could always probe for the weakest part of the examinee's intellect. In 1956, when he was particularly edgy from the demands of his double life, the doctor suspended a nurse from the school for an entire year because of the man's inadequate showing during an examination. The school had come to assume a central role in hospital society; suspension led to ostracism and ridicule. In calmer times, there never would have been a surplus of nurses willing to submit to the doctor's intensity; but they were all living in an extraordinary period that demanded leadership such as Fanon's. Enough of the nurses realized the nature of his achievements within the hospital as well as his contributions to the nationalist cause so that his service had ample numbers of hard-working Algerians. They had to be hard-working: There was no telling when the doctor, during one of his sleepless nights, would turn up at a pavilion to check on the work of the nurse in charge or to go over the notes on patients that other nurses had filed there earlier in the day.

Everyone knew that the doctor had a limited life expectancy at Blida. Because he was isolated from the other Europeans, it was assumed that Fanon was not hostile to the nationalist cause. Nor had he responded to the warning of Dr. Lacaton's case. As the F.L.N. stepped up its warfare, no corner of Algeria was immune from fear, terror, blood, reprisals. The planes again began taking off and landing over the hospital; police were back with loaded guns; nurses were disappearing into the *maquis* and into prison at a faster rate than before. Fanon's psychiatric work was continually disrupted; nor did he feel that his own contribution to the revolution was adequate. He decided to leave the hospital to work directly with the Algerians; but he wanted to turn the resignation itself into a political act. In late 1956 he wrote to the Resident Minister of the territory:

> During close to three years I have put myself totally at the service of this nation and the people who live in it. I have spared neither enthusiasm nor effort. There is not one bit of my energy which has not been directed toward the cause of creating a more liveable world.
>
> But what matters the enthusiasm and the care of one man if daily the truth is hidden by lies, cowardice, and contempt for mankind?
>
> What is the value of good intentions if their realization is made impossible by lack of spirit, sterility of ideas, and hatred for the people of this nation?*

Reading the letter out of context one might pass it off as some kind of self-congratulation decorated with noble clichés. Knowing Fanon's real attitude and work, however, one accepts it as very close to the truth. The doctor went on, in his letter of resignation, to explain the futility of trying to restore disturbed patients to a rational position within a society that itself was irrational. Fanon said that to remain in his present position of responsibility at Blida would constitute some sort of collaboration with the increasing French terror in North Africa.

Despite these feelings and the letter filed away in the office of the Resident Minister, despite the dangers to his own freedom, Fanon could not tear himself away from his work—he needed help from the French. In January, 1957, the doctor received an official "Letter of Expulsion"; he was given forty-eight hours to leave the territory or face arrest. The resident Minister's office had some sort of evidence linking him with "undesirable elements" in Alg-

* *Pour la révolution africaine,* pp. 59 ff.

eria. A letter like this was not to be taken lightly; it was perhaps a pardon from torture, two days of grace in which to escape a long prison sentence. Still, it is curious that Fanon was spared the more severe punishments handed Lacaton and so many of his patients. It was probably because Fanon's career was a little more advanced and his name better known. He had been offered other positions, one in Oran, and another, more recently, teaching neurology at the Faculté de Médecine at the University of Algiers. He had already published a good number of scholarly articles, and foreign publishing houses were seeking rights to his first book. Taken into custody, the doctor might have become a *cause célèbre*. There would have been new publicity surrounding the Algerian administration's methods of arrest, interrogation, and imprisonment. It was much wiser to throw Fanon out of the territory, inform Paris of the action, and leave further prosecution up to metropolitan officials.

In any case, Fanon and Josie packed up their books and clothes, prepared their young son, Olivier, for the trip, and left the sturdy, handsome, stone house where they had lived and worked for more than three years. Fanon's co-workers were aware of the gravity of the situation. Without exception all of his close associates, the Moslem male nurses, quietly disappeared from the institution on the same day that the doctor left. Within forty-eight hours after the arrival of the Letter of Expulsion, all three of Fanon's pavilions were without their usual supervisory personnel. The doctor was upset about his friends leaving their work, but he couldn't expect the nurses to subject themselves to the same kind of punishment from which he was escaping. It was a pretty sure thing that after his own departure the service would have been cleaned out.

The exodus seemed to confirm the other doctors' suspicions about Fanon's subversive activities. In late January, 1957, they could walk about the hospital grounds with smug looks of satisfaction: The place was theirs again. They could relax. They no longer had to be bothered with Fanon's newspaper, *Notre Journal*, which some felt publicized the lack of progress in their own services. Nor would the patients be given quite so much freedom any more. After all, the doctors' own families lived within the same hospital walls; earlier, several wives had complained about patients walking about the grounds, going to cafés, tending their own gardens without close supervision—without guards. There was a consensus among at least four of the European doctors remaining behind Fanon: The old order had to be re-established; things should be tightened up once again, if only for the patients' safety.

But there were two hundred other medical workers in the institution, mostly Moslem and mostly hostile to the doctors. Fanon had left his mark on them; the Letter of Expulsion increased his stature; even those who had been angered by his severe behavior remembered him as an outstanding doctor. Since the five *chefs de service* valued above all else their own leisure, it was the nurses and interns that were actually running the hospital. Fanon's reforms, for the most part, survived. The nurses still tried to perform their duties in the style the doctor had demanded; they continued to teach in their own school for younger medical workers. A photograph of Fanon somehow appeared on the wall of one of the lobbies of the nurses' residences. There was an occasional issue of *Notre Journal*—in a way the greatest tribute to Fanon's work at Blida. The colonialist doctors were too disinterested in hospital affairs to know that their subordinates were still printing the newspaper.

The Fanons returned to Josie's family in Lyons; but the doctor couldn't remain there long. Guy Mollet's Socialist government had tightened up internal security in all of France as part of the escalated war effort; Fanon could have been arrested at any moment. He planned to continue his medical work and writing in Tunis, headquarters for many of the revolution's leaders-in-exile. The voyage back across the Mediterranean represented no great decision for Fanon; he had joined the movement at an earlier date. Nor were the mechanics of the trip difficult: In the metropolitan territory there were at least half a million Algerian workers who devoted part of their time and a good deal of their salaries to the revolutionary cause; they were experts at secretly transporting men and arms to North Africa. Each large city and each department of France had its own F.L.N. office; new identification papers for Fanon were waiting in Paris.

His contact with the metropolitan organization was through the Professor of Philosophy Francis Jeanson who had written the Preface to *Black Skin, White Masks* in 1952. Jeanson was one of the outstanding figures in intellectual circles who had volunteered his service directly to the Algerian nationalists, and later was forced underground. Slight of figure, with a receding hairline and thick brown mustache, Jeanson might be considered a founder of the French New Left, which classified the Communist Party as just another variety of the national bourgeoisie. A veteran of the Second World War Resistance, Jeanson and his colleagues were part of a new *maquis* fighting against what it considered to be another variety of Nazism. Those working with Jeanson made a point of subordinating themselves to the Algerians running the war effort in North Africa; they took orders much more efficiently than most left-wing theorists. Jeanson saw to Fanon's immediate needs when the doctor arrived in Paris while they both awaited word from the Algerian contact.

In a later "Postface" to *Black Skin, White Masks,* the philosophy professor described his own relationship with Fanon as "businesslike." He wanted a closer friendship with Fanon—they had many matters to discuss—but was never given a choice in the situation. Jeanson wondered why the doctor always kept his distance. Was it that the war precluded such pleasures as friendship? No, Jeanson had always been close to a number of the Algerians with whom he worked in this period. Fanon, though, was quiet and self-contained; he seemed to want to end all conversations as quickly as possible. Jeanson at first thought that the doctor was shaken from his last months at Blida— waiting for a signal to flee from possible imprisonment or death. But eventually the professor realized that Fanon's coolness toward him was the result of his anxiousness to get back to work for the revolution. France, for him, was only the passageway to Tunis, where there was real work to be done. Fanon considered Jeanson nothing more than a *fonctionnaire* of the F.L.N. He didn't feel the necessity of being warm toward the professor who had helped to get his first book published and who was arranging for the voyage to Tunis; he couldn't spare the energy to be tactful. If Jeanson performed his own tasks quickly and efficiently, Fanon would be polite, nothing more.

VI
The Tunisian Front

Compared to Algiers, Tunis seems a homely and dull city. The Algerian capital snarls down at the sea from gigantic cliffs and high, rounded hilltops. Tunisia's major city was raised out of a mosquito-infested swamp five miles inland from the Mediterranean. Algeria is a large country with rich black soil: It attracted settlers in great numbers who planted their vines, fruit trees, and wheat and intended to remain there; Algiers became the pride of the French in North Africa. Tunisia's farming land is less fertile, the climate muggy; the exploitation was always more casual; there were fewer settlers; Tunis came about haphazardly at the crossroads of the area's major highways. The center of Algiers remained the Casbah with its baffling mass of crowded, narrow, winding allies, its stairways and dead-ended streets; its hundreds of shops offering to the city's Moslem population what we would consider exotic food products. In Tunis, the Casbah was renovated and made into a tourist attraction: The streets were widened, the buildings reconstructed; the food markets moved to other parts of the city; it catered exclusively to a Western clientele. The Tunisian capital was always more modern and efficient than Algiers, but without a North African personality.

Still, in 1957, when Fanon arrived there, Tunis had its own kind of fascination. Michel Deure, a U.P. correspondent, in Tunisia at the time, described the city as "absolutely insane." The U.P. office was in the Coliseum, a large complex of office buildings in the center of the city built around a courtyard with a huge open air café. In the daytime, according to the same reporter, the hundred-and-thirty tables there were occupied mostly by plainclothes police, journalists, intelligence agents, bodyguards, and revolutionary *fonctionnaires*. The city had two hundred "accredited" reporters; only thirty of them ever wrote newspaper or magazine articles; the rest were spies. The U.S. Central Intelligence Agency had a large staff in Tunis; so did the Russian K.G.B. Paris, of course, supported the greatest number of the clientele at the Café of the Coliseum: There were plainclothesmen from the French national police, agents from army intelligence, and men working for the Deuxième Bureau. There were free-lance spies too, supported by the Algerian right-wing terrorist outfits. The Algerian revolution, like all such movements, was split into factions; there had been some vicious infighting. The "Messalistes," followers of an older nationalist leader, were cleaned out of the F.L.N. ranks; but still, certain cliques within the revolution felt it necessary to keep tabs on each other. The secret police and body-guards of the various segments of the nationalist move-ment sat around the Coliseum also. In the evening, however, the hundred-and-thirty tables of the café slowly emptied out: The spies, agents, police, and guards were off to secret meetings all over the city. The journalists remaining behind were relieved that they wouldn't have to cover the evening gatherings.

The revolutionary personnel made their way to one or another of the hundred-and-fifty buildings owned or rented by the F.L.N. in all parts of Tunis. The Algerians, because of their efficient methods of raising money—from North African workers in France and from "revolu-tionary expropriations" in Algeria—were often richer than the Tunisians. The nationalists acquired some of Tunis' more elegant mansions, former homes of the most prosperous French settlers. These buildings served both as living quarters and offices; the locations of most of them were kept secret—from the Tunisian government too. The F.L.N.'s relationship with its host's administra-tion was a confusing and delicate ordeal. Tunisia had re-cently gained its independence from France; Bourguiba, the new head of state, was in complete sympathy with the Algerian revolution and wanted to give the F.L.N. every kind of support possible. He had at once sacrificed all French financial aid to the new Republic in order to con-tinue to help the war effort to the west. But Algeria was a much larger country than Tunisia; the Algerian national-ists had a more powerful movement than their counter-part in Tunisia. Bourguiba could never have raised an army the size of the F.L.N.'s; and he was just beginning to set up a police force in the new state. In 1957 Tunisia's

administration was so overwhelmed with the mess that the
French had left behind in their hasty retreat that the
F.L.N. operated there as an independent force. In Tunis
10 per cent of the entire population was Algerian. Had
open hostilities developed, Bourguiba could never have
expelled the Algerian nationalist without some kind of
foreign aid. Still, there was co-operation between the
Tunisians and their overextended guests. Both territories
had been the victims of long European occupations; the
Tunisians were anxious to aid the Algerians to escape the
rule of the French *colons* now evacuating Tunis itself.
There was almost a good-natured aspect to the revolutionary confusion within the capital city; there was a continual effort to work out agreements in the most
important day-to-day matters; everyone went on the assumption that the Algerian intrusion was on a temporary,
emergency basis, and necessary for the ultimate good of
both North African states.

Frantz Fanon held a number of different positions
within the Algerian revolution: He was a spokesman and
diplomat for the nationalists, he wrote for them, and he
was always working for the F.L.N. Health Service. Fanon
was at first a director of the Algerians' press service
in Tunis; in 1958, when the nationalists created a Provisional Government of Algeria, he was attached to the Ministry of Information. The press service, and later the
Ministry of Information, were located in a two-story,
dingy, white stucco structure not far from the Coliseum.
Fourteen rue des Entrepreneurs was the single important
address known to everyone who stopped at the coliseum's
café for a drink; it was the place where the revolution
surfaced; where its major policies were made known to
the public; where its changes in leadership were announced; where communiqués were given to the press;

where the revolution's newspaper was put together; where its radio programs were planned; where, after 1958, one had tangible evidence of the existence of the Algerian Provisional Government in Tunis. Fourteen rue des Entrepreneurs, like many of the city's buildings, had an inside courtyard covered by a glass skylight. The two floors of offices opened onto halls and balconies surrounding the courtyard, which was itself small, about thirty by forty feet. The revolution's public information was given out, at unannounced times, to those waiting in the courtyard. Each morning, a good percentage of Tunis' two hundred accredited journalists converged on 14 rue des Entrepreneurs; their reception hall, the small courtyard, was very poorly ventilated. On a bright sunny day, when the revolution was making news, temperatures within the Ministry of Information ranged upward to 120 degrees. The visitors were rarely in a good mood.

Perhaps it was a bit cooler and less crowded in the offices themselves where Fanon helped to write *El Moudjahid*. Earlier, this paper had been published in Morocco as nothing more than a tally sheet of the glories of the nationalist war effort. It seemed to be printed to reassure the revolutionaries that they were making progress. In Tunis, in 1957, the paper was reorganized into two editions: The Arabic one would deal more closely with specific problems and developments within the movement in Algeria; the French edition served both to keep Algerian workers in France informed of progress and setbacks in North Africa as well as to present the revolution to a much wider French reading audience in Africa and Eastern Europe.*

*The Yugoslavian government collected all of the issues of *El Moudjahid* between 1957 and 1962, and reprinted them in three bound volumes. Most of Fanon's articles are in *Toward the African Revolution* (New York: Grove Press, 1969). The quotations in this chapter are from the Yugoslavian volumes.

Redha Malek, the editor-in-chief, is a short, slightly over-weight individual with a lot of energy; when he talks he usually sits on the edge of his chair, cracking his knuckles, waiting for something more important to happen. He was well educated in French universities and is amazingly agile in politics; he has managed to hold important positions in each of the succeeding regimes of Algeria since independence. He is not an individual obsessed with ideology, but has a strong sense of self-interest—whether it be his own or that of his nation. His conversations with Fanon never could last too long because both of them were so articulate and so rapid in changing subjects; everything was out of the way in the shortest time imaginable. Malek also did a good deal of writing for *El Moudjahid,* and was a good critic of Fanon's prose because he could tame the doctor's excessive enthusiasm to make the article or the chapter of a book more effective. Malek could temper Fanon's idealism with talk of more immediate goals. On the other hand, Malek's efficiency was never enough in itself to produce a readable newspaper.

Doctor Pierre Chaulet came to work in Tunis too, and was made head of the F.L.N.'s *Centre de documentation.* He also wrote for *El Moudjahid,* and drew closer to Fanon because they were both, first of all, doctors. Chaulet, a lung specialist interested in new treatments of tuberculosis, was overworked in the F.L.N. refugee camps. The two doctors would run across each other daily in the nationalist health centers as well as in the paper's editorial offices.

Their newspaper was used to record the history of the revolution; at the same time, its articles give a clear account of the French counterrevolution. It was Fanon who recalled that at the beginning of the war, in 1954, the settlers depended on collaborators within the Moslem population to denounce the nationalists. But there weren't enough friends of the French; and the masses had little respect for the assimilated Moslems likely to aid the authorities. In the countryside, the Europeans resorted to a new method of attempting to isolate the revolutionaries from what they called the honest population. As mentioned earlier, Moslems were taken off their own small plots of land and confined in Relocation Centers—dirty, disease-ridden, crowded, prisonlike quarters. Moslems outside the centers could be shot as rebels. The relocated Algerians lost their livestock and crops; they were expected to work fortified fields using Western agricultural techniques without any explanation for either their new mode of living or farming. Those who escaped the Centers gained an understanding of one crucial factor: the necessity of rebellion.

As part of the counterrevolution, *El Moudjahid* explained, the French began to escalate what they called "psychological warfare." Propaganda was disseminated to try to exploit religious and regional tensions within the nationalist movement. Paid agents tried to spread rumors of the impending disintegration of the F.L.N. governing body in Tunis. Finally, the French army and police forces resorted to indiscriminate slaughter to produce an atmosphere where the masses might reject the revolution in order to live in peace again. At all times the Europeans operated in total ignorance of the extent and thoroughness of F.L.N. organization within Algeria.

The army, searching for reasons for its own impotence, decided that the revolution was inspired and supplied by certain foreign powers, the Communist bloc nations. In 1956, Guy Mollet's Socialist government, bowing to military pressures, invaded Egypt to try and cut off what they termed the major Communist supply route from the East. But the Algerian revolution continued on unaffected.

Egypt was in no way crucial to the nationalist war effort. Then, in May, 1958, the French army revolted against the Fourth Republic because it feared that the new Premier, Pierre Pflimlin, might appease Communism in North Africa—in other words, negotiate peace in Algeria. The generals felt they were saving France from Russian aggression. "Abandoning realistic decisions and decisive action," Fanon wrote, "the French in Algeria have taken refuge in wishful thinking and fantasies."*

In answer to the continued French propaganda on the war, *El Moudjahid* began to describe the organization of the revolution in some detail.† The nationalists had divided Algeria into six wilayas (political-military districts); metropolitan France was the seventh wilaya. Each wilaya had a number of zones; the zones were divided into regions; and there were smaller local sectors. Each of these divisions had one political and one military *chef* responsible to the appropriate command of the next larger area. In each zone the F.L.N. had a health service for the wounded and for Moslem civilians, social services for the families of those who were fighting or dead, and other administrative facilities. The financing of this complex network, and the raising of the money for the war itself, were the major tasks of the 400,000 Algerians living in metropolitan France. Money came directly from Algeria too: Ben Bella had begun his own revolutionary career supervising a $10,000 robbery of the Oran post office. *El Moudjahid* claimed that 75 per cent of the revolution's arms were taken from the French; most of the other weapons were purchased in West Germany. Whereas all of the F.L.N.'s arms were manufactured in the United States, the

---

*From Fanon's article in *El Moudjahid* (September, 1957).
†*El Moudjahid* (November 1, 1958).

French were using N.A.T.O. equipment against the nationalists.

Fanon's political education progressed rapidly as he wrote for the paper; Chaulet and Malek together were a gold mine of information on every detail of the history of the nationalist movement. There was a three-way dialectic; sometimes articles would emerge directly out of heated discussions. In 1958, M'hammed Yazid was named the new Minister of Information of the Algerians' Provisional Government; he was technically Fanon's superior. Yazid, like Malek, was another expert in tactics; he had been an advocate of Algerian independence since before the Second World War, forced underground in 1948. Yazid's war was of an earlier vintage than the F.L.N.'s, but he worked well in the new organization after 1954. He is a large man with slightly stooped shoulders and dark, thinning hair. He wears those gold-rimmed, tinted, highly polished glasses that provide European intellectuals with that not-to-be-trifled-with appearance. English, Arabic, and French flow from within him with impressive volubility; Yazid can get along in three other languages. He is married to an American whom he met during one of his official voyages to the United States. Talking with Yazid or Malek today one can sense a very slight resentment toward the enlarged reputation of Frantz Fanon. In their point of view, Fanon was something of a newcomer, a political personality formed by the Algerian revolution itself. This is perfectly true, but it possibly entails an underestimation of Fanon's contribution to the movement. It is somewhat the same kind of thing as Fanon's attempt to downgrade the work of Francis Jeanson, the professor in Paris who arranged his passage to Tunis. Fanon could never overlook the fact that Jeanson remained in France removed from the eye of the revolution. The Algerian leaders still think of Fanon, a black from the Caribbean, as an outsider too.

Soon after Fanon's arrival in Tunisia in 1957, there was a new effort to internationalize the Algerian revolution and increase pressures on France for withdrawal. Yazid, Malek, and others had been planning the campaign for some time; but Fanon was responsible for a large part of the propagandizing and some of the diplomacy too. *El Moudjahid* at first concentrated on presenting the revolution in its North African context. Algeria was economically and historically part of the Maghrib, the half-moon-shaped area of the coast including Tunisia and Morocco. These two states were already giving considerable aid to the revolution, but Fanon, in several articles, continued to point out that it was in their self-interest to give the aid. France was using economic pressure to try to influence the foreign policies of Tunisia and Morocco; she had cut off her aid to the two states because they had recognized the Provisional Government of the Algerian Republic. More important, French bombers had crossed over the border and wiped out the Tunisian village of Sakhiet Sidi Youssef while supposedly in combat with the F.L.N. Almost one hundred Tunisians had been killed.

> It is only with the coming of our independence [*El Moudjahid* stressed in December, 1957], that a Maghrib exploited for the needs of colonial strategy will give way to a unified and strong Maghrib capable of promoting the primary interests of the North African people.

None of the North African states would be free until all had thrown off French rule.

The nationalists' paper began to cover revolutionary activities in all of Africa, then the rest of the Third World.

Fanon found time to write on his homeland too. In 1957 the British Antilles were about to gain their independence; he argued that Martinique and Guadeloupe should reassess their position as "overseas departments" of France. Their close association with Paris seemed to have preserved all of the Antilles' economic weaknesses. As an independent state, the islands might seek new capital outside of France; they could diversify production, and have a wider market area. The wealth monopolized by the *békès* could be redistributed. The Antilles would have a chance to enter the twentieth century; Martinique could change from what Aimé Césaire had referred to as France's "island ghetto." The future of the Antilles had to be linked with coalitions of former colonial territories at the same stage of economic development.

Because of its expanded coverage and skillful editing, *El Moudjahid* had a tenfold increase in circulation in North Africa, West Africa, and Eastern Europe. The newspaper had to be moved out of the crowded Ministry of Information to its own separate headquarters. One indication of the paper's new prestige was the energy with which the French tried to forge issues. The army's Bureau of Psychological Warfare at first put out crude imitations that the nationalists enjoyed reading; the later forgeries were more serious problems. By 1960 psychological warfare, including the forgery projects, was the center of interest within the French military; the Bureau had greatly increased amounts of money available for all kinds of intrigue. In numerous articles in French military reviews, strategists explained the continued successes of the Algerian rebels firstly because of their aid from the "East,"*

---

*The French writers had to be vague on this aid from the "East"; statistical studies tended to prove the revolution was self-financed.

and secondly because the Communists had given them
extensive training in the use of propaganda and new psychological techniques to control the masses. It was necessary for the French to develop "counterpsychological"
resources to stop the spread of revolution. The French
army began radio broadcasting in Arabic; it published
special newspapers explaining the benefits of the European presence in North Africa as well as the disasters that
would come about with independence; and it set up a
cadre of traveling spokesmen, fluent in Arabic, who could
address informal town meetings and gatherings across
the countryside. The Bureau had to attempt to sabotage
the revolution's own means of communicating with the
people. In March, 1960, the French published a forgery of
El Moudjahid with normal reportage on the revolution except for certain small changes: a note that one of the
A.L.N.'s colonels had entered into private talks with the
French; another article exploiting regional and religious
differences within Algeria; a third mentioning that an independent Algeria would have to claim territory that was
part of the Moroccan state. The paper looked perfect; the
French had had the time and money to study *El Moudjahid's* distribution system. The phoney issues were eventually given out by the ordinary nationalist outlets; somewhere along the line the Bureau had slipped its own
material in before the regular issues arrived. Fanon's colleagues had to rush to put out a special issue of the real
El Moudjahid explaining what had happened; henceforth
distribution was more carefully guarded.

One morning, in the spring of 1959, Fanon met his assis-
tant at the Hôpital Charles Nicolle, Dr. Geronomi, another of the European settlers who had chosen to become
Algerian, and asked him:

"Could you take over the services here?"

"For how long?"

"Three weeks or so?"

"Sure. But could you tell me why?"

"I have to write a book."*

Geronomi didn't quite believe him, but within a month, Fanon had finished *L'An V de la Révolution algérienne* and was ready to submit it to a publisher. It was built about his notes from Blida, observations from Tunis, and hundreds of conversations with the rank and file of the revolution. This book, which Fanon originally wanted to call *The Reality of a Nation,* and which was distributed in English as *A Dying Colonialism,* was a study of the sociology of Third World nationalism, an attempt to publicize what had already happened in Algeria. The essays were an elaboration of the contention that the power of the revolution resided in the radical mutation of Algerian society after 1954. In five years a new nation had come to replace the North African French colony; it would only be a matter of time until the Europeans would be forced to give legal recognition to a *de facto* situation.

The Algerian women were emerging from years of obscurity to be part of the new nation. Fanon believed that the long-established subservience of Moslem women had been destroyed by the exigencies of war and revolution. They had clung to their traditional hooded and veiled clothing, always a symbol of social inferiority and domestic timidity, because of the European invasion of their homeland. The older kind of clothing provided a last barrier against the leering insults of the occupying forces. After 1954 women in the *maquis* discarded the robes and veil and, at the same time, were considered the equals of

*From an interview with Dr. Geronomi.

the males fighting in the guerrilla campaign. In the cities women gained new respect and equality as they too became engaged in the fighting: Their older flowing robes were useful for hiding weapons and bombs in urban terrorist activities. By 1958, the position of women was very much changed; in the new independent nation their political and social equality, according to Fanon, would become clear to all.

In Algeria today, however, a vast majority of women still dress in the robe and veil; they remain relegated to domestic lives. One hears stories of women who cut their hair and changed clothes to fight in the *maquis,* but returned home after 1962 to reassume the old clothing. At first glance, the present situation of women destroys the validity of Fanon's earlier essay. But this is not quite true. In the liberation period, many women were changed; those who fought, at least. There was the beginning of a genuine social and cultural revolution. At present, it appears that a great majority of Algerian males have turned against this revolution. As Claude Collin reported in *Les Temps Modernes:*

> . . . in the name of a return to Arab-Islamic values, alleging certain excesses which may have occurred, husbands and fathers managed to restore the veil.*

In the countryside, there is still a self-conscious retreat from the Western attitudes that the Algerians associated with colonialism. Fanon had underestimated the staying power of the traditional prejudices against the female sex (an attitude widespread in all of the Third World, but re-enforced by certain Moslem religious practices). It is

---

* Part of an excellent article on "L'Algérie An VII. Essai de description," *Les Temps Modernes* (November, 1969), p. 640.

only in the cities that female life today is somewhat improved over the colonial epoch. Within the middle class, women have gained substantial freedom: 35 per cent of the students at the university of Algiers are women; and Algerian women can now work as lawyers, doctors, and journalists. The cultural revolution that Fanon described existed—thus Claude Collin's interest in the subject—but it has lost the wartime momentum. Fanon himself was always worried that it would be difficult to sustain the strength of revolution after independence; his last book, *The Wretched of the Earth,* warns of the inherent dangers of a triumphant nationalism in the Third World.

Each essay in *A Dying Colonialism* addresses itself to a single factor in revolutionary life, but expands to give a picture of the whole nation coming to life. The first essay begins with a simple idea: that clothing reveals much about a group of people. Fanon then talks about the veil in the colonial period and within the war. The nationalists, in less than five years, had succeeded in unveiling a substantial number of Moslem women, something that the French had tried unsuccessfully to achieve for more than a century. At the Blida hospital, Fanon had found that women would not leave their wards unless they were allowed the veil. Within the revolution, women themselves discarded the veil. The role of women in the nationalist movement sets off a chain reaction in Fanon's head: the essay goes on to describe what the revolution can do in other areas of life.

The second chapter of *A Dying Colonialism* is concerned with another detail of everyday life, the radio. Before the Second World War, 95 per cent of all radios in Algeria were owned by Europeans. All broadcasting was in French. Radio Algiers, a subsidiary of the French national radio network, had programs suitable only to the interests of the 10 per cent settler minority. The broadcasts were trying to convince the Europeans in the cities that they lived in one of the more important provinces of France; Radio Algiers served to reassure the *colons* in the countryside that they were not isolated amidst the Moslem masses. The Moslems themselves ignored the radio. At the hospital at Blida, Fanon had more than one patient, though, who considered the radio mysterious and evil; it was almost a phobogenic object. After 1956, however, the radio became one of the more important weapons that the nationalists used against the French.

Before the radio, and before *El Moudjahid* had wide distribution, the F.L.N. depended on French newspapers to disseminate information to the masses. In 1954, there was a small European left-wing press in Algeria that carried news of the nationalist movement other than that distributed by the French army and Algerian administration. The liberal newspapers printed in Algiers, Oran, and Constantine had wide distribution within the Moslem community; those who could not read French were able to hear accounts of the most important developments from bilingual friends. But this press was an early victim of the repression; the *colons* and army shut down all of the publications left of center. Henry Alleg, editor of the *Alger Republicaine,* was taken into custody and tortured by the police; civilian vigilantes had destroyed his offices and presses.

During 1955 the only way the Algerians could have definite information about the F.L.N., aside from personal contacts, was through the more liberal metropolitan newspapers and periodicals that arrived in North Africa's larger cities. Certain of these journals increased their circulation in Algeria fivefold. Soon, though, the purchase of *L'Express, Le Monde,* or *Humanité* became dangerous; Moslems buying these publications were subversive; it was enough of an excuse for a police officer to make an arrest. Finally the European news dealers refused to handle any of these newspapers or magazines; their response to customers asking for them was uniform: "That filthy stuff doesn't come to Algeria any more."

El Moudjahid was first printed in Algiers as an attempt to fill the information gap, but its offices were discovered and presses destroyed. A new paper was set up in Morocco, but distribution in Algeria became a complex and dangerous task. When Fanon helped to reorganize *El Moudjahid* in Tunis, the newspaper was more important to the revolutionaries in exile. But then Radio Free Algeria, using the facilities of the Egyptian radio network, began to broadcast the paper's news to the Algerian masses. Three weeks after wall posters and leaflets announced the regular nationalist broadcasts, all the stores in Algiers were sold out of radios. In rural areas, groups of Moslems would pool money to buy one transistor set; in 1957, there was a rush on radios throughout the territory. Radio Free Algeria was able to set up its own transmitters and expand broadcasting in Arabic, Kabyle, and French. The listeners felt part of the new nation. Again the strongest proof of the effectiveness of Radio Free Algeria came from the French: In 1957 the army banned the sale of all kinds of radios in Algeria without speific police permits for their purchase. After this, the nationalists had to set up new supply lines to get radios into the territory from Tunisia and Morocco.

Radio Free Algeria and its millions of clandestine listeners attested to "The Reality of a Nation." Before Fanon's book, there were few people in the metropolitan nation who knew of the existence of nationalist broadcasts in Algeria; nobody knew about the upsurge in radio sales.

Skeptical readers could check on Fanon's work by doing
a bit of research; radio manufacturers had statistics for
sales in North Africa. The army's regulations banning the
sale of radios were public. It was obviously not the *colons*
that were responsible for the huge upsurge in sales; nor
would the army have been concerned if the new purchas-
ers were listening to French programming. Fanon's thesis
was indisputable.

In another essay in *A Dying Colonialism* Fanon describes
the attitudes and the goals of the European doctors who
had come to Algeria after 1950—the same gentlemen
whom he had worked with at Blida. The Moslems, in general, reacted unfavorably to the new sanitary laws and
treatment that were pushed upon them without any kind
of explanation and without their consent. The same kind
of medicine, when supervised by Algerians within the
context of the revolution, had brought much more favorable results with the same patients. Fanon could speak with
some authority on this subject because after 1958 he acted
as a medic within F.L.N. troop installations along the
Tunisian-Algerian border. He treated civilians as well as
soldiers: Their attitudes, he explains in the essay, were
very different from what he had seen at Blida.

A Dying Colonialism concludes with a chapter on the divisions within the one million European minority bloc in
Algeria. After describing the extensive interests of the
richest *colons,* the attitude of the urban middle class, and
the discrimination practiced against the Jewish segment
of settlers, Fanon gives, in lengthy direct quotations, the
personal accounts of two Europeans caught up in the
revolution. One of them, Bresson Yvon, a police officer
stationed near Sétif, had been sharply criticized by his
superiors for having too many Moslem friends. After
1954 Yvon had to stand by while the same friends were
tortured and murdered:

Algerians were chained between two trucks which would roll slowly in opposite directions, the officer said. Then there were the regular tortures with water and electricity; men would be strung up by their thumbs, or by their testicles.*

Out of repulsion, Yvon joined the F.L.N. and became a secret agent within the police. He found, in the police archives, a long list of Moslem suspects who were supposed to be informally executed by the police. Shortly after he passed a copy of the list to the F.L.N., he was removed from duty, tried, and given a five-year sentence in prison. Since there hadn't been any conclusive proof that Yvon was guilty—only his former friendships— the authorities were relaxed in the punishment handed down.

Fanon, working for the Ministry of Information and with numerous contacts within Algeria, had obtained the police officer's own account (under a pseudonym) of his changing position in the Algerian social order. "I have done these things because I'm Algerian," Yvon concluded, "I don't feel as though I'm a traitor to France. I am an Algerian. . . ." Yvon's testimony, and the other personal account that precedes it, are given as footnotes to the contention that the settler bloc was not homogeneous or monolithic. The revolution could work within European quarters too. In one sense, Fanon's book was a retaliation against French psychological warfare. The French had tried to promote dissent within the ranks of the F.L.N.; Fanon was attempting to widen cracks sometimes visible in the colonialist front. The last section of *A Dying Colonialism* could also be considered as laying the groundwork for some future *rapprochement* between the

---

*From *A Dying Colonialism* published under later French edition of yet another title, *Sociologie d'une révolution* (Paris: Maspero, 1968).

Europeans and the Moslems within an independent Algeria.

The book did not live up to Fanon's hope of inciting world-wide support for the Algerian Revolution. Paris had effectively closed the avenues of communication from North Africa to France and the rest of the world. In the metropolitan territory there was both an official and an unofficial censorship of material from the revolution. The larger commercial publishing houses, such as Editions du Seuil, which had published *Black Skin, White Masks,* would not accept material of the nature of Fanon's new essays; they didn't want to risk a hostile public reaction to what amounted to a bitter attack on the French war in North Africa; they didn't want to be accused of aiding the enemy, Moslem nationalism, or Communism. Fanon's new house, Maspero, was the one strong voice of dissent in the publishing industry during the war. But the newspapers and literary journals boycotted all of Maspero's books; they weren't important enough to be reviewed, just propaganda. . . .

The only newspaper in all of France to discuss *L'An V de la Révolution algérienne,* when it was published, was *Au Progrès de Lyon.* The reviewer in Fanon's university town called the book "a manual for use by the cadres of the F.L.N." The quarterly reviews also ignored the book. Not a word from *L'Esprit,* the first periodical to publish Fanon's works in France. A bit later, *Le Monde*'s Third World expert, Jean LaCouture, expressed the orthodox liberal interpretation of what had happened to Fanon:

> I admired his talent and his coverage, but after having greatly appreciated the first book, I found myself in profound disagreement with the theses that he presented afterward. . . .

It had been fine when Fanon expanded on the psychiatric underpinnings of Western racism in *Black Skin, White Masks,* but later when he began to act against the political and social evils of the same society, and report on the experiences of action, the community of liberal analysts remaining behind somehow felt betrayed.

Maspero's books were distributed through certain left-wing bookstores in Paris and other large cities; the young editor had a large following in student circles. For some in France *L'An V* was the first experience with the major social changes that had already taken place in the North African countryside. For others, this was the first detailed account of the tortures and murders in Algeria that had leaked through to the metropolitan territory. Fanon's name became associated with the concept that if one did not participate in the war against colonialism, one would become the colonialists' accomplice. In this period more and more university students were taking the risk of working for the F.L.N. in France: raising money and helping one another escape the draft. An indication of the importance of Fanon's book is that after six months of circulation the Paris government, operating with special emergency powers, ordered all copies seized. Further printings were prohibited. The Maspero catalogue, with *L'An V de la Révolution algérienne* halfway down an impressive listing of already-banned books, was all that remained of the doctor's essays. But he had predicted:

> Crushing the Algerian revolution, isolating it, suffocating it, exhausting it . . . these are all absurd dreams.
> The essence of the revolution, the true revolution which changes mankind and renews a society, is

much further advanced than that. The oxygen which brings about and sustains a new kind of human being —that too is the Algerian revolution.*

* *Sociologie d'une révolution* (Paris: Maspero, 1968).

VII
The Oxygen of Revolution

In Algeria, when Fanon himself first tasted "the oxygen which brings about and sustains a new kind of human being," he had to conceal the effects. The enemy was all about. It was later in Tunisia that the intoxication became evident. It is difficult to write about his activities after 1957; one can't do them justice by organization into separate, and what would have to be artificial, essays. Describing his days as they unfolded, though, would result in confusion and disbelief; each was filled with highly organized, if unimaginably diverse, projects and creations in three different phases of the revolution. A journalist, he also published books. He was a psychiatrist who was called upon on occasion as a physician. He had helped in the architectural renovation of an F.L.N. health center where he was also an administrator. In his last years, Fanon was the most distinguished of the revolution's permanent representatives in black Africa. All the while he attended numerous meetings within the Ministry of Information in Tunis; he traveled to Tripoli for plenary sessions of the revolution's parliament (the nationalists went to Libya to escape the increasing concentrations of intrigue in Tunis). Fanon was an F.L.N. delegate at Pan-African conferences throughout the continent; he was appointed the revolution's ambassador to Ghana. His days became a *mélange* of responsibilities; his schedule inhuman.

Still, Fanon had an ample number of friends with whom to share evenings of good food and good liquor. The nurses at Blida and Tunis cannot imagine Fanon drinking —he was so serious during work hours—but other friends love to describe his abilities to relax, talk about music, complain about less than perfect food, appreciate fine *digestifs*. Dr. Charles Geronomi remembers one evening in Tunis with the Fanons and several other medical colleagues: By 11 P.M. the women were wearying of the steady drinking and fast conversation; they were beginning to doze off in the living room. Fanon, though, kept the men talking as he continued to fill glasses around the circle. After 2 A.M. the doctors began to collect their sleeping wives to get home for a bit of rest. The host kept protesting, making fun of their weariness. Geronomi, younger than Fanon, couldn't make his escape till four in the morning. The next day he limped into the Hôpital Charles Nicolle, late for the morning shift, to find that Doctor Fanon had already been there for an hour. Fanon seemed genuinely perplexed at Geronomi's slow pace that morning.

Traveling as a diplomat for the F.L.N., Fanon cemented new friendships: Félix Moumie, a nationalist leader from Cameroun; Patrice Lumumba from the Congo; and Roberto Holden from Angola. Older acquaintances visited him in Tunis. Bertold Juminer, a medical doctor and also the head of the left-wing political opposition in French Guiana (the small territory south of Martinique on the South American mainland), would go swimming with Fanon and his wife on the beaches of Carthage outside of the city. Fanon was sometimes very rough on these older acquaintances: When they met each other for the first time in several years in 1958, he snarled at Juminer:

> Well, still playing at politics in Guiana and the Antilles? You know, one of these days a kick in the ass from France will force you to fight for your independence. You'll owe it all to Algeria, the territory that used to be the prize whore of the colonial world.*

The conversation went on from there with Fanon easing up slightly on his attack. Even on the Carthage beach, however, he seemed unable to forget politics—except to discuss existential philosophy, which for him was a basis of politics. Fanon gave his friend a copy of *L'An V de la Révolution algérienne* with the inscription:

> This book is the illustration of a principle: action is incoherent agitation if it does not serve to reconstruct the consciousness of an individual. The Algerian people, in the great struggle that they lead against colonial oppression, bring to light their own

*Quotations from Juminer in *"Hommages à Frantz Fanon," Présence Africaine,* 1er trimestre (1962), pp. 118–141. Juminer's interpretation of the friendship, however, is different from the one presented here.

national consciousness so that an Algerian nation, based on mass participation, can no longer be deferred. Have confidence in your people and devote yourself to helping them re-establish their dignity and spiritual awareness. For us, there can be no other choice. . . .

Fanon's dedications were never to be taken lightly; they were basic revelations about his own way of life. There was usually a deadly serious intellectual core to Fanon's closest friendships.

It was said that if someone insisted on being warm to Fanon, talking to him and boring him, he would get up in the middle of the conversation and leave the room. His tolerance for small talk appeared greater with attractive women.

If, on the other hand, somebody made a statement that Fanon found to be fundamentally wrong, he was not satisfied just to contradict it. The false contention had to be refuted, but more important, *destroyed.* His furious rebuttal quite often demolished not only the original statement, but also the person who had had the misfortune to let it slip out. In Tunis, Fanon gained a reputation for fierce social hostility. In 1959, Giovanni Pirelli was in the city collecting documents for a new study on the revolution. The Italian author was impressed by *L'An V de la Révolution algérienne,* and wanted to meet the doctor. The *fonctionnaires* in the F.L.N. Ministry of Information told Pirelli not to bother; he was white and European; Fanon wouldn't have time for him. When they did meet, Fanon kept baiting him, but with no reaction. Pirelli, experienced in left-wing politics, wasn't going to argue over minor points because it was clear that he and Fanon were of one mind in their contempt for the inaction of the largest segment of the European left. As Fanon realized that Pirelli's book was part of the campaign to internationalize the revolution, the hostility dwindled; by the time of their second meeting, they were friends. Pirelli wrote a very thorough factual account of the doctor's life in the introduction to the Italian edition of *L'An V* in 1963.

I asked Pirelli why he never expanded his introduction into a full-length interpretive biography. He replied:

> I've thought of it. I even sat down, once or twice, to write a longer essay on Fanon. But you know, I got to know him pretty well. I remember his face, and his attitudes. Each time that I begin to venture an opinion on Fanon, I feel as though he's standing in back of me, looking over my shoulder—angry. It's those glaring eyes . . . I'm never able to go on.

Perhaps Fanon discussed more intimate and personal matters with Pirelli and Juminer, but always their talks rolled around to politics, usually the politics of Third World independence. One time, when Juminer was with him, the news arrived in Tunis that the French national police had just killed three Martinicans during a very minor disturbance in Fort-de-France. Fanon took Juminer's hand; he was jubilant over the dispatch:

> They should use the victims [he spat out at his friend], they should air them, and parade them through the villages and cities in open trucks. . . . They should shout at the people, "Look at the work of the colonialists." But they won't do any of this. They'll vote symbolic motions of censure and go into mourning. In the end, this mild show of anger serves to reassure the colonialists. It's a matter of releasing pent-up tensions, a little like certain erotic dreams. One makes love with a shadow. One dirties the bed. The next day, all is in order again. All is forgotten.

Fanon's favorite method of relaxation remained blazing discussions that would last throughout the whole night by their own momentum. He had no conception of time, only of interests. He could contaminate others with this impulsive volubility. A friend of his in Tunisia described an evening when he, Fanon, and two others sat in a darkened room around a table with a small lamp in the center. Fanon had become extremely intense; so had the other three at the table. The doctor created sparks of nervous energy about himself. He could always listen but vastly preferred to talk. He had on a sport jacket and polo shirt open at the neck. Fanon was almost always beautifully dressed: His shirts were tailor-made in Europe; the hottest Tunisian summer day couldn't deter him from modeling a new, heavy tweed suit. That night the lighting in the room accentuated the depth of the many creases in his face and the jaggedness of the scar on his left cheek. Fanon's eyes, usually bloodshot from lack of sleep, burned out of dark wells. At times; he would think with his forehead resting on clenched fists, elbows on the table. Then he would lift his head, squint his eyes, relax them, and speak while occasionally rubbing his nose vigorously.

He was talking that night about the doctors in charge of the hospital where he worked in the suburbs of Tunis. After 1957 Fanon was also a civil servant of the Tunisian state, a *chef de service* in the government's Psychiatric Hospital at Manouba. The Tunisians were aware of Fanon's dual responsibilities within the Algerian revolution; he was welcomed at Manouba because the institution had been deserted by its French staff immediately after independence. Though its methods of patient care were somewhat advanced over those at Blida in 1953, Fanon was not at all satisfied. Manouba had quite extensive facilities for work therapy, its own newspaper, and considerable freedom of movement for the patients in the wards; but the hospital also had a large population of what were referred to as the "chronically ill"—treated as though they had received a life sentence to a prison-hospital. There were none of the more subtle refinements that Fanon had brought to Blida—cafés, excursions outside the hospital, patients' gardens, and such. When Fanon began to press for changes, he ran into the unbending opposition of the Tunisian doctor in charge of the institution. M. Ben Soltan, fifty years old, with a big belly and tiny hands and feet, was more conscientious in attending to hospital duties than M. Kriff at Blida; in fact, Fanon's new superior was always inspecting matters within the hospital; and, in a short while, scrutinizing Fanon's service.

Though educated in France, Ben Soltan had been a strong Tunisian nationalist since his student days. Once Tunisia had gained its independence, he felt his mission as a radical was fulfilled. He wanted to preserve European methods of patient care within the hospital. Doctor Ben Soltan considered himself a socialist, and this meant that the state should control the larger industries, public transportation, and health facilities in his nation. But he didn't believe in the equality of peoples: Not all of his countrymen had the same intelligence and abilities; not all had received the benefits of a French education. Ben Soltan was convinced that Tunisia needed a superstructure of administrators to direct the lives of the masses: Order and hierarchy were necessary to construct a modern state. The director believed that those well up within the hierarchy, like himself, had to be accorded certain small privileges in their private lives, merely as compensation for their enlarged responsibilities. Most of all, the administrators needed absolute authority over their subordinates; without that, progress would be impossible.

The director of the Psychiatric Hospital at Manouba resented the Algerian intrusion into the affairs of his new state. Half of the twelve hundred patients within his own institution were Algerian; many of his nurses were Algerian; and one of his *chefs de service* was tied up with the revolution. The Algerians were slowing down Tunisia's economic development and making his own job more difficult. Nor could the director express this opinion publicly; the Tunisian government was officially friendly to the revolution. Ben Soltan was not only educated in Europe, he thought like a European, and he served as a perfect model for the kind of attitude that Fanon attacked in his essay, "The Pitfalls of National Consciousness," in *The Wretched of the Earth.* The director was a member of a group of Third World nationals who had stepped into the positions vacated by European colonialists:

> To them [Fanon wrote], nationalization quite simply means the transfer into native hands of those unfair advantages which are a legacy of the colonial period.*

The hospital director, and his friends, Fanon said later, had come to power in the name of a narrow kind of nationalism—as evil, in its own ways, as European colonialism. They were actually overseas representatives of phony Western liberalism devoid of any genuine humanist content. The doctor's own relationship with the director of the Manouba Hospital was a disaster. On his first visit to Ben Soltan's office, Fanon presented the plans for completely modifying his service within the institution; he recommended that the other *chefs de service* at least consider the validity of his proposals for renovating their own

---

The Wretched of the Earth, p. 152.

pavilions. Fanon didn't ask Ben Soltan's opinion of the plans; he assumed that he had complete authority to do as he wished in his own service; he was there only to request increased funds for extended work-therapy facilities. The director was speechless over the audacity of his new subordinate, and angered over the doctor's trampling over fine hierarchical barriers; but Ben Soltan did not feel competent to discipline Fanon during their first meeting. He put him off with a more simple tactic: There was no money available. Fanon wanted to know why not (he was used to ample financial assistance during his years at Blida; funds had never been a problem there). The director answered that the Tunisian Minister of Health had already alloted the budget for the coming year to the hospital, and that was what they would have to work with. Fanon wanted to know if Ben Soltan could ask increased funds for what the doctor considered crucial reforms. The director felt that such a request would be challenging the Minister's competency to judge—something unpermissible in an underdeveloped country, where order and hierarchies were the prerequisites for progress. Fanon's reply was that he himself would talk to the Minister; he had no idea that he had just smashed the most sensitive spot in the director's pudgy psyche. He was outside of the administrative center before Ben Soltan appeared able to react. A nurse in the center at the time remembers Ben Soltan bursting out of his office in an indescribable fury, rushing off to find other Tunisian doctors so that he might explode about the outrageous conduct of the new black *chef*. He had forgotten to tighten his tie and put on his suit jacket; it was the first time that the nurse had ever seen the director in the hallway in his shirt-sleeves.

After lunch that day, on his way to the *El Moudjahid* office, Fanon called on the Tunisian Minister of Health, who was a much more relaxed and secure type than Ben Soltan. The Minister respected Fanon's dynamic informality; they got along well together. It was true that there was no possibility of expanded funds for the hospital; the state was still running on what might be termed a crisis budget, but Fanon received a promise of support for an effort to rearrange the finances within his institution in order that some innovations could be put into effect. The news of this success with the Minister of Health convinced the director at Manouba of the necessity of continuing to build a coalition opposed to the projects of the new *chef de service*.

Although he had no taste for pseudonyms, Fanon worked at Manouba under the name of Dr. Fares. He followed normal F.L.N. procedure in the matter. After the publication of his second book, it was necessary to go underground a bit deeper. Dr. Fares and his family moved into a spacious apartment within the large administration center guarding one side of the entry to the Manouba complex; Doctor Ben Soltan's office was in the other wing of the center. Manouba lacks the view of blue mountains that is part of the beauty of the hospital at Blida, but still it has its huge shade trees, velvety green lawns, stone benches along carefully tended flower gardens, and dozens of small, bright-looking buildings for the medical services. One thing that could be said of the Europeans in North Africa: Their insane asylums were extremely tastefully designed. But most of the elegance was for the enjoyment of the doctors alone—just as the other "benefits" of colonialism accrued only to the colonizers. Fanon's first tour of the luxurious grounds seemed a repeat performance of his entrance at Blida. He ordered bars removed and doors unlocked in all of the four pavilions under his charge. There were few patients in strait jackets, but he advised the nurses that he wished all of the patients free of such restraints as soon as possible. Tunisia, however, was still having difficulties getting the new tranquilizing drugs from the West.

The doctor's first major reform project again brought him into battle with Monsieur le Directeur. Fanon had followed up his conversation with the Tunisian Minister of Health by obtaining a copy of the hospital budget, which showed that a good part of the finances were going toward the upkeep of the "chronically ill," the Tunisians who had been stashed away by their relatives in the hospital for over a decade. He began to interview these patients with the greatest of care to find out if it was really necessary to keep them at Manouba. In the majority of cases it appeared as though they would be capable of leading more normal lives outside of the institution. Many of the "chronically ill" had been so thoroughly trained in their work-therapy sessions that they could find good positions in the new nation with its shortage of skilled labor. Fanon calculated that the hospital could eventually release up to two hundred people. This would free considerable amounts of the budget for other uses, and allow for the admission of more serious cases. M. Ben Soltan, when confronted with Fanon's plans, pronounced them unworkable. A short while before, another young doctor there had wanted to release large numbers of the long-term patients. The director, because of his own insecurity, went to the Minister of Health to have him rule on the matter. With his compulsive cautiousness, and because he feared jeopardizing his own administrative record, the director had not presented the doctor's case forcibly. The Minister could not therefore, in good conscience, endorse the project. Ben Soltan used this earlier interview as his grounds for vetoing Fanon's plans. He seemed to be pleased to be able to give the doctor a flat refusal.

Hammed Ben Salah, the Minister of Health, was an old-time trade-union man in North Africa, one of the more radical of the Tunisian nationalist leaders. He knew that Fanon's professional career was well advanced and had been pleased with his original offer to work at Manouba. They had gotten along well at their first meeting. At the second, Fanon bore down on money matters. He showed the Minister figures on what might be done with the funds going to support the patients he wanted to release; Fanon also had plans for a new outpatient department to keep in touch with these cases. The minister was quickly convinced; he would talk to Ben Soltan about the matter.

During the last months at Blida, and in Tunis, Fanon continued an exhausting program of medical research. In 1956 he contributed a highly technical paper to a medical conference of psychiatrists and neurologists at Bordeaux; in 1957 he had another such publication in a Moroccan medical journal.* At the same time, he was working on medical articles with wider social implications. With Dr. Sanchez, he completed a short essay on the attitude of North African Moslems toward insanity.† It was an introduction to a planned longer study (never completed) in

---

*"Le T.A.T. chez la femme musulmane. Sociologie de la perception et de l'imagination" presented at the Congrès des médecins aliénistes et neurologues de France et des pays de langue française; "Le Phénomène de l'agitation en milieu psychiatrique. Considérations générales —signification psychopathologique," *Maroc Médical* (January, 1957), pp. 21–24.
†"Attitude de musulman maghrebin devant la folie," *Revue pratique de psychologie de la vie sociale et d'hygiène mentale*, No. 1 (1956), pp. 24–27.

The three Fanon brothers—Joby, Félix, and Frantz—the forward line of the St. Pierre (Martinique) soccer team, 1946–47.

Courtesy Studio Kahia.

Fanon at an F.L.N. press conference—Tunis, 1957.

Courtesy Studio Kahia.

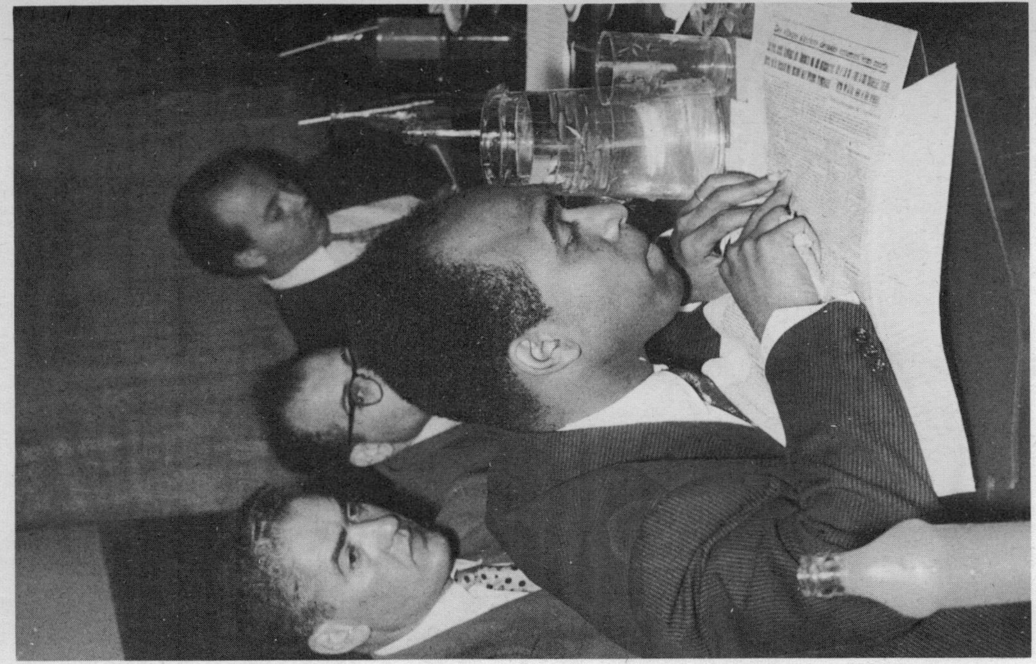

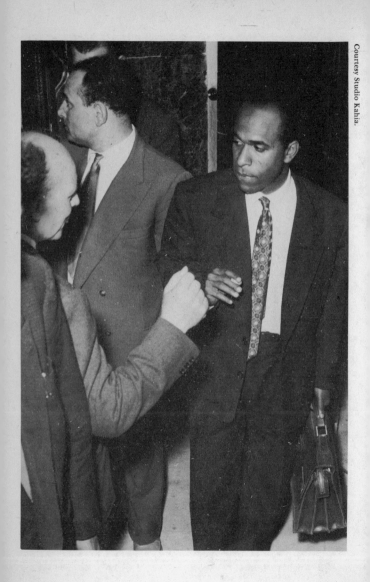

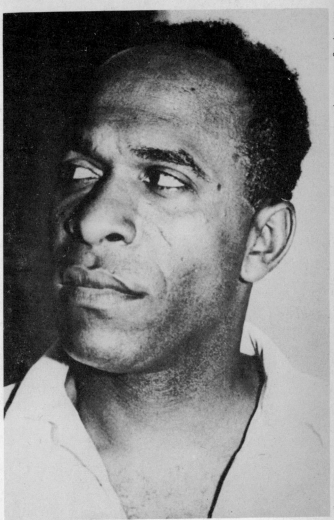

Frantz Fanon in 1959.

A page from Fanon's diary during his African excursion to open a southern front for the Revolution, eventually published as *Toward the African Revolution*.

The issue of El Moudjahid with Fanon's obituary.

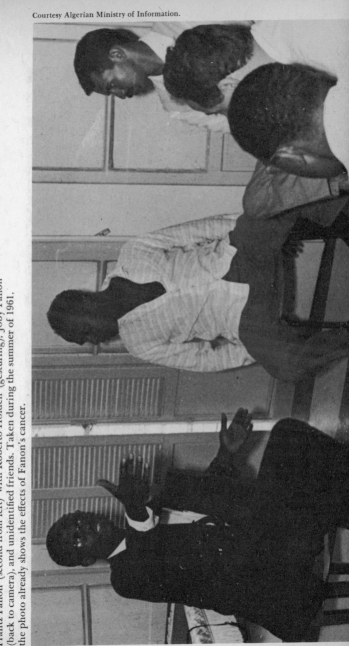

Courtesy Algerian Ministry of Information.

Frantz Fanon (second from left) with Roberto Holden (gesturing), Joby Fanon (back to camera), and unidentified friends. Taken during the summer of 1961, the photo already shows the effects of Fanon's cancer.

Fanon's funeral–December 1961. F.L.N. soldiers bear the casket into Algeria.
The tall civilian on the right with hands clasped behind his back is O. Iselin.

which the two doctors compared the Western tendency to hold the insane accountable for their behavior to the North Africans' belief that insanity was caused by outside forces beyond the control of the individual, family, or community. The Moslems' attitude had resulted in better treatment for the insane at earlier times. There had been institutions comparable to modern insane asylums before the middle ages in North Africa. In some instances, however, the insane were thought holy or elevated to sainthood, which tended to retard modern therapy.

By 1959 Fanon was able to submit the results of his largest research project for publication in Tunis.* This involved his opening a day-care psychiatric center, with eighty "beds," at the city's Hôpital Charles Nicolle. The center was designed to further Tosquelles' concept of restoring therapy to its proper social context, but also to deal with the overflow of cases and scarcity of doctors and facilities typifying the Third World nations. The idea of a day-care institution for the insane was not new; Duncan MacMillon had pioneered such a center decades earlier in Nottingham, England; still, in 1959, there were only twenty of these existing in the world. Fanon's was the only one in Africa—in fact, in all of the Third World.

With the support of the Tunisian Minister of Health, Fanon had renovated an older psychiatric service at the Hôpital Charles Nicolle: The pavilion had been repainted in more cheery colors; all of the old "systems of security" were done away with. The new patients themselves, organized into teams, helped to remove the grillworks from windows, demolish the walls separating the older isolation cells for inmates, and take apart the huge locks on

*F. Fanon and C. Geronomi, "L'Hôpitalisation de jour en psychiatrie. Valeur et Limites," *La Tunisie Médicale*, No. 10 (1959), pp. 689–732.

every door. These same patients would arrive at the center each day at 7 A.M.; the nurses would greet them (one nurse for six to eight patients), and after breakfast interview them as to what had happened in the twelve hours between their departure and return. The nurses were expected to keep full notes on patients' dreams, anxieties, relations with their families, sleeping habits, and other troubles. The nurses would also give brief physical examinations, taking the patients' temperatures, blood pressures, and so on. The rest of the morning was given over to therapy.

The patients included psychotics, paranoiacs, and those suffering from temporary nervous breakdowns. Shock treatment and insulin therapy were used in certain cases; others were psychoanalyzed; still others received behavioristic (Pavlovian) therapy. The afternoons were used for work therapy, sports, and recuperation from the strains of the morning's treatment. The patients were all dismissed at 5:30 P.M. The families had exact instructions on the medical care for those who had been subjected to shock or insulin therapy; there was an emergency telephone open at all hours in the hospital. Occasionally a patient was advised, but never forced, to spend the night in the hospital. In a little over a year Fanon and his colleagues treated one thousand patients; less than 1 per cent had to be sent to Manouba for more permanent hospitalization; the rest were dismissed as cured. The term "cured" might be clarified: Psychotherapy within the Third World had to serve a more basic purpose than in the West; successful treatment would allow a patient to continue to function in his social environment with some minimum of happiness. Fanon and his colleagues could not afford the time to supervise a thoroughgoing program of psychoanalyses. At the beginning, the patients were staying at the center for an average of fifty-three days; when Fanon and his younger colleague, Geronomi, wrote an article about the center, this average had been reduced to twenty-six days. None of those in treatment, or released from the center, had been involved in accidents related to their state of mind.

What were the advantages of a day-care center? First of all, Fanon showed, it cost much less money per patient treated. Secondly, it allowed the patients to remain in their ordinary social and familial contexts. This made therapy easier. Doctors could more quickly ascertain what factors in these contexts were contributing to the illnesses. The patients didn't lose touch with society; their hours were much the same as working hours; they could easily be reintegrated into their normal social existences as the cure progressed. In other hospitals where Fanon had worked there had never been therapy for more than eight hours a day—this could be accomplished at the day-care centers. The doctor came to believe that full-time hospitalization was necessary for only the tiniest fraction of all the cases he had reviewed; he advocated strict new legislation to protect the rights of the others. Fanon regarded day-care centers, such as the one established in Tunis, as a very practical solution for many of the severe problems of treating the mentally ill within underdeveloped nations. There was less of a need for new large psychiatric institutions than for smaller, more moderate psychiatric day-care centers.

At the Hôpital Charles Nicolle, and Manouba, Fanon still got along better with the nurses than the doctors. Though he had more than three hundred patients at Manouba alone, Fanon could keep informed about the progress of each through the nurses' detailed notes. One time, examining the records of a doctor, his subordinate at Manouba, Fanon threw them across the table snapping, "Where did you get these? They aren't true." The doctor named the nurse from whom he had taken the notes. Fanon called in the nurse and examined his notebook. It turned out that the doctor had recorded the wrong observations for the wrong patient. Fanon severely disciplined him with the nurse still present. He maintained that the doctor was intoxicated with the sole concept of getting ahead. He cared little about the quality of his day-to-day work because he was thinking only of his advancement within the hospital hierarchy. The doctor had forgotten about others, such as his patients; he exhibited a capitalistic greed for success.

There is not enough evidence left of Manouba's day-to-day operations to determine if Fanon's lecture was justified; quite often, though, he jumped to conclusions from small bits of data. And always, his impatience with less than perfect performances aided the director, M. Ben Soltan, in recruiting support for his campaign of revenge. In conversations among themselves, the doctors in Ben Soltan's camp referred to Fanon as "the Nigger." There were always new reasons for hostility toward this *chef de service*. Summer in Manouba is even hotter than in Blida; temperatures quite often go above 100 degrees Fahrenheit. It is a strong custom there, and in most of Tunisia, to work from seven or seven-thirty in the morning till one in the afternoon; then to quit for the day. If exceptionally ambitious, one would work again after five in the evening. Fanon could never accept such a relaxed schedule; he didn't think about the heat. The doctor worked through the afternoons. Fanon was well-liked by the patients; his publications had made him the most distinguished *chef* in the hospital; despite his rigorous standards, the interns chose to work for Fanon before the other doctors. Most of the other *chefs de service* described Fanon's energy as a form of exhibitionism; they resented his popularity.

Though small in spirit, Ben Soltan was a clever man. He could not use medical reasons to fire this doctor whom he and his colleagues hated, since there were extraordinary evidences of Fanon's achievements within the institution. Almost three hundred patients had been released without any kind of serious incident afterward. Ben Soltan instead tried to dismiss Fanon for political reasons. In 1959, the director accused Fanon of being an undercover agent spying on both the Tunisians and Algerians for the state of Israel! He was to be ousted from the hospital as a Zionist and a threat to Tunisia's internal security. The case against Fanon was built on his writings, for example his first book, where he had said:

> Anti-Semitism hits me head-on: I am enraged. I am bled white by an appalling battle, I am deprived of the possibility of being a man, I cannot dissociate myself from the future that is proposed for my brother.*

The dossier against Fanon maintained that he was part of a Jewish clique in the hospital that was continually having secret meetings. (It had worked out that way: Often when Fanon called a staff meeting to discuss changes in hospital policy, only the two Jewish doctors on the staff cared to attend.) Secondly, Fanon had been visited at Manouba by some European doctors; they, too, were Jewish. (Fanon's medical reforms, though very basic and not entirely original, were attracting attention in Europe. Some young Italian interns had come to Tunis to interview him. Perhaps

Black Skin, White Masks, p. 88.

they were Jewish.) Thirdly, Fanon was continually arriving at the hospital, and leaving it, throughout the night. Fourth, the doctor entertained an inordinate number of people in his apartment. His guests came at all hours of the night. Fifth, Fanon had been away from the hospital for long periods in 1959. (He was on official F.L.N. missions.)

The dossier against Fanon, which probably sounded quite impressive to the doctor's enemies, was laughed out of existence by the Tunisian Minister of Health. Fanon was reinstated before the dismissal took effect. Yet he couldn't work at the hospital with the same energy as before; he transferred his major effort to the F.L.N. health centers. The Fanons left their apartment in the large white administrative center of the Tunisian hospital to move to one of the F.L.N.'s secret addresses in Tunis.

In Fanon's last years of life, the great enemy was the new bourgeoisie of the Third World—the businessmen in charge of the sector of the economy that had escaped nationalization, as well as the higher civil servants, and the technicians in charge of the state industries. This bourgeoisie, according to Fanon, lacked the dynamism and real power of its Western counterpart. The European and American middle classes were at least a highly trained and sophisticated caste with a powerful ideology. They had accumulated enough wealth to insure a minimum of prosperity in their own nations—enough to stifle class consciousness among the workers. Fanon apologized, in his later writing, for even using the term bourgeoisie when referring to the Third World's upper stratum. More accurately, they were a greedy, voracious group of hucksters who hoarded insignificant amounts of power and money. "It remembers what it has read in European textbooks," Fanon said of Ben Soltan's class, "and imperceptibly it

becomes not even a replica of Europe, but its caricature."*

In 1959 *L'An V de la Révolution algérienne* was published.
Fanon was still writing for *El Moudjahid,* and practicing
medicine at seven different locations. In the Bey's Palace
he concentrated on developing his new, but very simple
"sleep cure." So many of the war's casualties were nervous breakdowns caused by overexhaustion and sustained periods of extraordinary tension that Fanon often
judged extended therapy unnecessary. Partially because
of the shortage of doctors but also because the patients'
ailments were the result of unusual social circumstances,
they were encouraged to attempt to cure themselves.
Given a more easy environment they could regain their
senses almost automatically. Fanon would begin by pre-
scribing a week's sleep, natural sleep if at all possible,
otherwise a sedated rest. The patients would be up only
two or three hours a day, for meals and a leisurely stroll
through the hospital gardens; then back to sleep. When
the prolonged deep sleep was not enough to effect a
regression of the symptoms, other therapy would begin.
Sleep alone had been enough to revive the stability of Si
Saddek, the A.L.N. commandant hidden in Fanon's own
home in Blida. The sleep cure was also successful for
some hundred other cases in the health centers around
Tunisia.

The greatest problem was always numbers: too many
patients, too few doctors. Nowhere was this more pressing than in the F.L.N. refugee camps strung out along the
Tunisian and Moroccan borders of Algeria. There were
some quarter of a million Algerians living in unspeakable

* *The Wretched of the Earth,* p. 175.

poverty and misery there. On his periodic tours of the
camps, Fanon had to be both physician and psychiatrist;
but still he could not adequately cope with the immense
amount of work awaiting him. He tried, for instance, to
give therapy to groups of women suffering from puer-
peral psychoses, the name given to mental disorders in
and around the period of childbirth, but he had to conclude:

> . . . the fundamental nature of these problems is not
> cleared up by the regression and soothing of the dis-
> orders. The circumstances of the cured patients tend
> to cause the reappearance of the pathological
> disabilities.*

The camps were overcrowded; there was no decent housing or sewage disposal. There was no chance of employment or even work therapy. Worse, French aviation
frequently crossed the borders pursuing nationalist soldiers; certain camps had been bombed and strafed. The
refugees were always in fear. . . .

During a trip to a camp on the Moroccan-Algerian border, Fanon's jeep was blown up.† Miraculously escaping
death, he had twelve fractured spinal vertebrae. The lower
half of his body was almost totally paralyzed. He was flown
back to Tunis, then to Rome for more specialized medical
treatment.

---

*My own translation of the notes appearing on p. 279 of *The Wretched
of the Earth*.
†There are strongly conflicting accounts of this incident. Two Algerian
doctors working with Fanon in Tunis claim that there was no explosion, but a serious automobile accident. Other friends of Fanon claim
that there was a bomb in his car—part of an assassination attempt from
within the revolution. Fanon's own doctor mentioned the jeep being
blown up by a land mine. For lack of other concrete evidence, I've
accepted the story of Fanon's doctor.

The F.L.N.'s representative in the Italian capital received a telephone call to meet the doctor's plane at the airport. Before he reached his car in the street, there was a terrific explosion. The automobile was demolished, two children playing in the street were killed.

There had been a time bomb in the car's engine that went off prematurely. An attempt on Fanon's life, evidence showed it to be the work of the Red Hand, an organization of right-wing settlers from Algeria who had decided to contribute what they could to the war effort by selective assassinations and counterterrorist bombings in both North Africa and Europe. The Red Hand had to its credit two attempts at murdering the German arms dealer Otto Schlueter (who sold American weapons to the F.L.N.); a more successful sabotage effort against a German ship carrying arms to North Africa; the November, 1958, assassination of Ait Ahcene, the F.L.N. representative in Germany, and more than ten other attacks on those co-operating with the Moslem nationalists. It was hard to define the exact links between the Red Hand and the French administration and army in Algeria, except that the settler terrorists had access to highly detailed information on the F.L.N. as well as inexhaustible supplies of the powerful dynamite derivative known as *plastique.* More convincing, the Red Hand evolved into the *Organisation Armée Secrète* (O.A.S.), a larger and more desperate terrorist outfit headed by French army officers and former members of the Bureau of Psychological Warfare.

In any case, Fanon made it to the Rome hospital safely. The next day, however, glancing through an Italian newspaper, he noticed a small article announcing his arrival there, and giving the number of his room in the hospital. It was the kind of informal invitation to murder so frequently handed out by governmental secret-service bureaus. Agents could plant such articles, through contacts with the press, and allow civilian terrorists to take care of the execution. Fanon demanded that his room be changed. That night, two masked men entered his old, darkened room and sprayed the empty bed with a Browning automatic. Fanon could never afford to be amused at the incompetence of the Red Hand.

The violence was not in his head or just in his writing —but all around him. It was hard to distinguish the violence of the French settlers from that of the army, except that the military had the means to kill on a larger scale. Whereas the police had come down hard on the F.L.N. network in Europe, the Red Hand seemed to be operating with impunity: more documentation for the assertion that Western society, especially Western colonialism, was permeated with violence. Colonialism could only be destroyed with violence. In all the years of nationalist warfare, however, and in the nationalist peace that followed, there were never camps of French refugees bombed by F.L.N. aircraft. Those who attack Fanon's passages on violence have not considered the scale of killings. More than 10 per cent of Algeria's Moslem population was obliterated in the course of the French retreat to the northern shores of the Mediterranean.

VIII
Black Africa

The 1960 All-African Peoples Congress in Accra, Ghana, had a plenary session with long speeches by leaders of African nationalism from all over the continent. Nothing of great importance was being said. The audience was getting that overly relaxed sensation that is often induced by large congregations of important academics. The announcement of the next speaker, the representative from the Algerian revolution's provisional government at Tunis, did not startle the listeners out of the creeping somnolence encouraged by the tens of thousands of words floating over and about their ears. The speech itself was a different matter. As recalled by Professor Peter Worsley from England:

> I found myself electrified by a contribution that was remarkable not only for its analytical power, but delivered, too, with a passion and brilliance that is all too rare.*

With the audience now impatient to hear each train of thought finished, the representative, Frantz Fanon, stopped suddenly, in the middle of the speech. He appeared overcome. He could not go on. His speech had been startlingly different from the cool, analytical performances that had come before it. Everybody stopped with Fanon, waiting for him to regain strength. The auditorium was astonishingly quiet. Fanon's pitch of emotions had spread over the normally calmer persons surrounding him. When he was able to speak again, the audience seemed relieved.

Worsley met the speaker and was able to inquire what had happened during the session. Fanon replied that while he was speaking he had begun to think of the killing, torturing, and suffering of the war that he was in. He felt inadequate to convey to those before him the extent of the sacrifices of the Algerian people. Nor did he think it necessary: The F.L.N.'s cause should have commanded the automatic support of all people who had tasted colonial domination—in fact, the support of all rational people. He had been unable to continue speaking because of the tearing sensation within him. And in the end, he had conveyed these feelings to the audience as much by the emotional interruption as by the script of the speech.

Since the days of the defense of his medical thesis at Lyons, Fanon had been an effective public speaker. After

---

*From Worsley, "Frantz Fanon, Evolution of a Revolutionary," *Monthly Review* (May, 1969).

1956, at the same time that he began to work with the nationalists, he took on lengthier engagements before more varied international audiences. Increasingly, the listeners could feel that his passion, sympathy, anger, and hatred were genuine; they became susceptible to the rhythms of the talks. He was soon one of the chief verbal propagandists of the *Front de Libération Nationale* outside of Algeria, and was named as a delegate to most of the international conferences of independent Third World powers after 1958. One can see in his speeches a sustained effort to relate cultural and social matters to Third World political developments as well as the changing theories of the role of nationalism in this part of the globe.

His first major speech, before he was in the F.L.N., was given at the Congress of Black Writers and Artists held in Paris in September, 1956. The meeting was dominated by an older generation—Fanon's teacher, Aimé Césaire; Léopold Senghor, the head of the Senegalese Republic, to whom Fanon once applied for a job; Richard Wright; the Haitian writer, Jacques Alexis; and Alioune Diop, the editor of *Présence Africaine*, the largest black publishing concern. It was Diop who gave the first speech expanding on the French concept of "assimilation" and the harm it had done to indigenous African cultures. Fanon picked up the same theme in his own lecture; however, the doctor at first adopted a style that managed to obscure his contentions. In the crowded Sorbonne lecture hall, thick with cigarette smoke and heavy autumn heat, Fanon began:

> The unilaterally decreed normative value of certain cultures deserves our careful attention. One of the paradoxes immediately encountered is the rebound, egocentric, sociocentric definitions.*

*Quotations here and following from *Présence Africaine* (June–November, 1956), a special issue devoted to the congress. James Baldwin, too, gives a description of the general atmosphere at the Paris meeting in

For his first performance before a distinguished international audience Fanon had worked over the speech to a point where some of its language was self-conscious and awkward, propped up with social science jargon. He was using the language of the societies under attack. Still, his ideas, in 1956, were important. He showed how European and American intellectuals had been drawn into the habit of evaluating varied world cultures according to the technical advancement of the societies under study. Western superiority was continually documented—by those doing research in the social sciences and humanities too. This made it easier to justify the continued expansionist policies of Western governments. The scholars had inadvertently constructed hierarchies of cultures, based on introverted technological values, with the lighter-skinned peoples' civilizations in a domineering position. It had not been possible to enslave the rest of the world without making it logically the inferior. Racism, for Fanon, was only the emotional expression of what the scholars and technicians had achieved in their own work.

The 1956 speech became more specific; but the transitions were abrupt. Suddenly Fanon was talking about the wide extent of racism in the northern United States as well as the South—a social fact documented by black militants in the country a decade later. The Southerner in the United States was not an emotional freak, but the most obvious indication of the true thoughts and feelings of the expansionist, domineering American society:

A society has race prejudice or it has not. There are no degrees of prejudice. One cannot say that a given country is racist but that lynchings or extermination camps are not to be found there. The truth is that

Nobody Knows My Name, pp. 13-55. Fanon's speech is reprinted in *Toward the African Revolution*, pp. 31-44.

all that and still other things exist on the horizon.
Their virtualities, these latencies circulate, carried
by the life-stream of psycho-affective, economic
relations.

Fanon's '56 speech is most original in its assumption that
American blacks can be classified, in sociological studies,
with the colonized of the Third World. These "racialized"
peoples, as Fanon terms them, recovering from the first
onslaught of Western brutality, the nineteenth-century
wars of conquest in the Third World as well as slavery in
the Americas, want to adopt themselves entirely to Western styles of life:

> Because no other solution is left to it, the racialized
> group tries to imitate the oppressor and thereby to
> deracialize itself. The "inferior race" denies itself as
> a different race. It shares with the "superior race" the
> convictions, doctrines, and other attitudes concern-
> ing it.

The speech to the Congress of Black Writers and Artists
seemed to follow the pattern Fanon established for the
development of the colonized cultures. Beginning with a
stultified, artificial language appropriated from the Western academics, Fanon's style changes suddenly; his own
language takes shape; words flow more easily; meanings
are clearer. The social sciences format has collapsed. Fanon is vivid:

> Having judged, condemned, abandoned his cultural
> forms, his language, his food habits, his sexual
> behavior, his way of sitting down, of resting, of laugh-
> ing, of enjoying himself, the oppressed *flings himself*
> upon the imposed culture with the desperation of a
> drowning man.

Cool, logical development, carefully structured paragraphs—all this gave away to a kind of writing and speaking reminiscent of Nietzsche's aphorisms. Individual sentences catch the audience's, or the reader's, attention; while they are being pondered, Fanon has rolled on to totally different topics. In 1956 he suddenly began to map out the future course of the Black Power movement in the United States, the resurgence of cultural nationalism, the resurrection of an African style:

> This [precolonial] culture, abandoned, sloughed off, rejected, despised, becomes for the inferiorized an object of passionate attachment. There is a very marked kind of overvaluation. . . . the oppressed goes into ecstasies over each rediscovery, the wonder is permanent. Having formerly emigrated from his culture, the native today explores it with ardor. It is a continual honeymoon.

Fanon, at this early date, was discussing an issue that has split black militants apart in the United States today: the politicized groups as opposed to those dedicated to reconstructing separate black societies.

Fanon always stressed that the real basis of racism was economic and political. Racism was a decoration for oppression and exploitation. Although blacks might at first have reacted to white racism with another kind of racism, this was not the most promising solution. There was nothing original about black racism; it ended as a caricature of the white perversion. Fanon maintained that the blacks's struggle had to take place on a markedly more human level:

> The perspectives are radically new. The opposition is the henceforth classical one of the struggles of conquest and liberation. Racism is not the whole but

the most visible, the most day-to-day and, not to mince matters, the crudest element of a given structure.

To understand the originality of Fanon's concepts in 1956, put yourself back in the United States in that period. Two years earlier the Supreme Court had ruled on the necessity of school desegregation. Martin Luther King, Jr., headed the largest party of progressive blacks in the country, and they, along with a small number of idealistic white college students, were beginning to confront the medieval racism of the South. There was only a tiny element of radical black nationalists, Robert Williams and a few others, mostly followers of Marcus Garvey, who realized the true extent of racism throughout America, and who considered passive resistance an inadequate response to unrestrained repression. The Black Muslims were becoming a small, powerful movement but primarily within the prisons. Malcolm X, in 1956, was beginning to preach under the guidance of Elijah Muhammad. At the same time that Fanon was depicting the superstructure of racism atop expansionist capitalism, Malcolm was warning:

> I know you don't realize the enormity, the horrors, of the so-called *Christian* white man's crimes. . . . Not even in the *Bible* is there such crime! God in Wrath struck down with *fire* the perpetrators of *lesser* crimes!*

While Fanon was explaining the intricacies of what we call "nativism," the retreat backward into older cultural habits in the face of the invasion of a new, hostile civilization, Malcolm X was stating:

* *Malcolm X Speaks* (New York: Grove Press, 1968).

God has given Mr. Muhammad some sharp truth. It is like a two-edged sword. It cuts into you. It causes you pain, but if you can take the truth, it will cure you and save you. . . .*

The example cannot diminish Malcolm X's demagogic brilliance or the importance of his later social criticism, but it helps to recreate Fanon's context. His thoughts of the 1950s are central to black politics of the 1960s. *Soul on Ice* might be described as Fanon coming home to roost. Eldridge Cleaver's writing, though refreshingly original, has that clarity of thought reminiscent of the Martinican rebel fighting within the Algerian nationalist movement. When Stokely Carmichael left the Black Panthers because of their willingness to work with white radicals, Cleaver advised him:

An undying love for black people that denies the humanity of other people is doomed. It was an undying love of white people for each other which led them to deny the humanity of colored people and which has stripped white people of humanity itself.†

In 1956, Fanon's speech, touching on the same subject of black racism, was lost in the deeper shadows cast by Richard Wright and Léopold Senghor. James Baldwin, in a detailed report on the Congress made no mention of the Martinican doctor. The First Congress of Black Writers and Artists operated under severe limitations. Paris was hardly an ideal location for the meeting. The French capital was central to all attempts to preserve the nineteenth-century map of the African continent. Blacks from the

*Ibid.
†"An Open Letter to Stokely Carmichael," *Ramparts* (September, 1969), pp. 31 and 32.

West African colonies could not speak freely there; Fanon, from Algeria, had to cloak some of his more important points in literary allusions. There had been a general agreement to ban political discussions at the Congress; but politics was foremost in the delegates' minds. Political and economic repression were discussed at great length, but always as to their effect on cultures. Baldwin observed, ". . . the 'cultural' debate which raged in the hall was in perpetual danger of drowning in the sea of the unstated."*

Présence Africaine was the sponsor of the Second Congress of Black Writers and Artists held in Rome three years later. Although Alioune Diop hoped that an important part of the proceedings would be centered on art and literature, the political crises around the world monopolized the speakers' thoughts. There was a much larger war raging in Algeria; a number of the other African colonies were pulling away from French domination. With the decline of W.E.B. Du Bois' generation in the United States, there was the growth of a new variety of black nationalism. Malcolm X had traveled to Mecca, his social and political views razor sharp, their impact too great for Elijah Muhammad's pleasure. There had been a broadening of black coalitions across international lines on the most general issue of all, the one that Fanon had stressed earlier, the oppressed versus the oppressor. Fanon could claim little direct responsibility for the developments; but he had pointed in the exact direction of the increasing tension.

In 1959 the radical leadership of Black Africa was shared by Kwame Nkrumah, President of Ghana, and

*Baldwin, *op. cit.*

Sekou Touré, who had led Guinea out of the French neocolonialist network called the "Community." Touré gave the keynote address to the Second Congress; and Fanon quoted from it in *The Wretched of the Earth:*

> To take part in the African revolution it is not enough to write a revolutionary song; you must fashion the revolution with the people. And if you fashion it with the people, the songs will come by themselves, and of themselves.
>
> In order to achieve real action, you must yourself be a living part of Africa and of her thought; you must be an element of that popular energy. . . . *

Touré expresses the same kind of existential revolutionary philosophy that Fanon lived by: It was never sufficient to observe social upheaval from the outside; the most penetrating social analyses would be a by-product of participation in the upheaval.

Fanon's speech, following Touré's, was a further refining of the themes proposed in 1956. During the nineteenth and twentieth centuries, Fanon began, the Europeans had consciously, and accidentally, wiped out all traces of older civilizations in Asia and Africa. Colonial ideology profited from this obliteration by impressing upon the colonized the depth of their own barbarity and the dangers of being thrown back to pre-European nothingness. Without the superior governments, cultures, and technologies of the West, the natives would be in horrible difficulties. Independence was tantamount to nonexistence. Fanon said:

*The chapter, "On National Culture," in *The Wretched of the Earth,* which begins with this quote from Touré, is built around Fanon's 1959 speech at Rome. The speech itself is included as the last part of the essay. The quotations that follow are drawn from this chapter as a whole.

Colonialism did not seek to be considered by the native as a gentle, loving mother who protects her child from a hostile environment, but rather as a mother who unceasingly restrains her fundamentally perverse offspring from managing to commit suicide and from giving free rein to its evil instincts.

In Europe's eyes, there were no Angolans, Sudanese, or Ghanians—only natives. The continent was a vast, amorphous conglomeration of jungles and deserts inhabited by a "race." The ideas of *négritude,* and of a universal black culture, Fanon re-emphasized, came in response to the white man's original notions of Africa. *Négritude* is the antithesis of the colonial view of black life, and therein lies its weakness. *Négritude,* as first explored by Léopold Senghor and Aimé Césaire in the 1930s, was important as an ideological refutation of the French concept of assimilation, but noticeably obsolete during the national liberation struggles of the 1950s. In the United States it was the patriotic white Christians who brought to life Black Muslims, but by the time of the Black Panther movement in the 1960s, the Muslims were slightly obsolete. The Moslem bourgeoisie in North Africa, Fanon found, was often as racist as the American middle class. Repression and exploitation were universal features of Western society and Western colonialism; but they had to be dealt with on a national level. The specific challenges facing Negroes in the United States were totally different from those facing the blacks south of the Sahara. The tasks to be performed within independent and progressive Guinea were miles apart from those within occupied Portuguese Africa. In the colonies, national liberation wars were the first stage of the struggle against Western barbarism.

In the liberation period there were new national cultures coming to life from the pulse of the awakening peoples. There was no need for the black intellectuals to dig back to precolonial times in order to find archaic precedents for the outpouring of art. The scholar who remained in the archives apart from the battle against colonialism would, in fact, return to his culture as a foreigner. The final proof of a nation was not in the resurrection of an older civilization but in the movement against the forces of occupation. What Fanon describes, in the end, is not a black culture, not an African culture—not even a national culture—but a revolutionary one. He was certain that the important Third World art was a product of the struggles for independence. The style of the art was harsh, Fanon explained, and full of images,

> for the image is the drawbridge which allows the unconscious to be scattered on the surrounding meadows. It is a vigorous style, alive with rhythms, struck through and through with bursting life; it is full of color, too, bronzed, sunbathed, and violent. This style, which in its time astonished the peoples of the West, has nothing racial about it, in spite of frequent statements to the contrary; it expressed above all a hand-to-hand struggle and it reveals the need that man has to liberate himself from a part of his being which already contained the seeds of decay.

The art of Fanon's own essay serves to illustrate his theme. Once he is in the Algerian revolution, his writing loosens up; he makes larger generalizations. Everything speeds up. He offers wilder, but more original ideas. Fanon gets carried away, "struck through and through with bursting life." The conclusion to the chapter "On National Culture" is a huge outpouring of a liberated intellect, roaming without inhibition across large panoramas of cultural developments. In order to clarify his interpretation of the growth of Third World cultures he delves into highly varied forms of art, from literature to pottery to storytelling. He describes changes in the narrative tradition at the time that the revolution spread across the Algerian countryside. The Moslem storytellers who had for years related inert, ancient episodes modified their presentations after 1954 to deal with the contemporary upheaval. Very specific incidents in the new guerrilla warfare were put into dramatic form without revealing names or places. Each time that the storyteller related new information from the revolution he also presided over an original dramatic creation. The tension of the production spread to his public. The nature of almost all storytelling performances changed: Comedies disappeared, as did tales of troubled individuals and tormented consciences. The new tales dealt with actions and repercussions. The common man could understand this drama more easily. Audiences became larger but more compact; it was as if they had to be closer together to participate in the conspiracy. The storyteller was giving freer reign to his imagination. A new art form resulted. The French authorities attested to the vitality of the art, its effect on the public, by arresting a large number of the traveling storytellers, who had existed quite peacefully in earlier colonial times.

The art of woodworking in Algeria evolved during the revolution. For years, in one part of the territory, there had been a standardized, carved decoration of a highly stylized mask with a rigid body beneath. All kinds of furniture and paneling were embroidered with this same ornament in the colonial period. By 1956, the faces being carved on the masks had changed: They appeared to be coming to life; they had different expressions. There were new bodies, in motion, beneath the masks. One could find compositions with several bodies, the portrayal of action.

Standardization was a thing of the past. In ceramics, too, the older formalism was abandoned. The numbers of colors of pottery increased; bright ochers and shimmering blues had been developed.

Fanon believed that the appearance of new kinds of jazz, even rock-and-roll, were signs of the growing restlessness of the blacks in the United States. The passing away of the classical jazz period marked the beginning of another struggle against racism and oppression. There were distinctive art forms that typified peoples reconstructing themselves. Art, as well as ideology, grows from action—or else reflects inaction and repressive situations. A national culture, Fanon maintained, is the whole of the efforts made by a people in the sphere of thought to justify and praise the action through which that people creates itself and keeps itself in existence.

Fanon's essays on Third World cultures emerged, as one would suspect, from his involvement in the area's politics, his interest in Pan-Africanism, and his activity in the Algerian war.

> To put Africa in motion, to cooperate in its organization, in its regrouping, behind revolutionary principles. To participate in the ordered movement of a continent—this was really the work I had chosen.*

He was intent on opening a new stage in the Pan-African movement by beginning the integration of radicalism north and south of the Sahara. Theories of Pan-Africanism had developed rapidly after the First World War. The movement began in the United States under W.E.B. Du Bois, as a protest against racism and colonialism. Du Bois organized five Pan-African conferences between 1919

*Fanon's notebook in *Toward the African Revolution*, pp. 177 and 178.

and 1945 that were attended by the more radical students from the African colonies studying in Europe and the United States. The nature of the meetings changed from panel discussions on the wretched conditions for black studies in the West to an organized drive for decolonization itself. Nkrumah and Jomo Kenyatta were two of the more impressive nationalist leaders emerging from the early stages of Pan-Africanism. Through the 1950s there was always a serious contradiction within this movement: Whereas the term "Pan-African" referred to the unity of the continent, and the community of interests of blacks throughout the West, the better-known leaders of the movement were successful nationalist figures thoroughly involved in their own country's affairs. They could afford little more than verbal support for other, less advanced liberation struggles.

Fanon might be considered a Pan-African "revisionist"; he attempted to impress Africa with the importance of the Algerian war at the same time that he spoke of the limits of the older plans for continental unity. He wanted to lay the groundwork for more meaningful Pan-Africanism after national independence. His work within the movement consisted of speeches, an effort to expand communication among the more radical nationalist leaders on the continent, and a campaign for the recruitment of an all-African army. Fanon's last years were spent publicizing the dangers of neocolonialism, emphasizing that political independence could mask more subtle economic manipulation by renovated Western interests. He considered a certain degree of African unity essential to give social, economic, and cultural substance to the post-colonial epoch.

In December, 1958, Fanon was in Ghana's capital, Accra, as part of the F.L.N.'s five-man delegation to the

African Peoples' Conference. He chose the occasion to speak and write on the subject of violence and decolonization. It was the same year that the French had revamped their African empire into "the Community," providing for a referendum in each territory so that the inhabitants might endorse the local leaders' wishes to remain affiliated with the metropolitan territory. Guinea, under Sekou Touré, was the only colony to demand full independence. Still, the French had accorded all the territories a kind of political self-determination; the colonies were now considered semi-autonomous national units. Because of this, a number of delegates at the Accra Pan-African conference argued that revolutions were unnecessary; national independence was on its way—peacefully. It became Fanon's task to remind his African colleagues that the improved conditions in their colonies were a result of the warfare north of the Sahara. France had not the resources, in 1958, to cope with nationalism in Black Africa. De Gaulle had been shrewd enough to keep one step ahead of the independence movements—but always with the notion of preserving whatever French interests he could in the various territories. History, Fanon emphasized, shows that no colonial power will retreat without exhausting all possibilities for maintaining its rule:

> Nonviolent decolonization is less a sign of some new sense of humanity in the colonialists than an indication of the pressure of a new ratio of forces on an international scale.
>
> It is clear that France has begun a process of decolonization south of the Sahara.
>
> That this has occurred without violence can be attributed to the successive setbacks of French colonialism in other territories.*

* *El Moudjahid* (December 24, 1958).

In Accra and elsewhere Fanon discussed the dangers of neocolonialism. He put forth the thesis that France, unable to compete industrially with the other nations forming the Common Market, had offered these states her African colonies as investment opportunities—in return for concessions protecting underdeveloped French commerce in Europe. French colonialism, changing to neocolonialism, had to become "European" to survive. The members of the Community in Africa would automatically become Associate Members of the Common Market, a step that could in no way benefit their beginning industrialization. The specter of the West was everywhere; the Europeans still physically occupied large expanses of the continent; and in the independent nations, according to Fanon:

> . . . the United States had plunged in everywhere, dollars in the vanguard, with [Louis] Armstrong as herald and American Negro diplomats, scholarships, the emissaries of the Voice of America. . . . *

As the Algerians' delegate to various Pan-African meetings, Fanon came into contact with Patrice Lumumba, who was at the head of the nationalist drive within the Belgian Congo; Félix Moumié, from the Independence Party in the French territory of Cameroun; Tom M'Boya, fighting for Kenya's independence; and Roberto Holden, laying the groundwork for a guerrilla campaign against the Portuguese in Angola. Fanon denied that he considered individual personalities overwhelmingly important in left-wing political movements, but still, these were the leaders, along with Nkrumah and Touré, whom he felt capable of understanding the necessity of African unity in

* *Toward the African Revolution*, p. 178.

the postcolonial era. Fanon thought in terms of a loose federation of the more progressive states that could pool resources for more important politico-military drives, such as freeing Portuguese Africa, or extracting reparations from Western colonial powers. There was the beginning model of this sort of thing, in economics at least, in the new trading union set up between Guinea and Ghana. Before applying himself to any kind of larger federation, Fanon set to work on what he considered the crucial project of an African legion of volunteers to fight first in Algeria, then in the other colonialist strongholds to the south. He had to engage in a kind of informal diplomacy as he traveled about the continent attempting to convince the various nationalist leaders to contribute men and material to a supranational cause.

By 1959 the French had built two new Maginot lines along Algeria's Tunisian and Moroccan borders. Of course Maginot's architecture had been renovated: Electronic surveillance equipment replaced the troop bunkers and fixed cannons; helicopters were more efficient than the older underground tunnels. The new technologies of fortified "no man's lands" had drastically reduced the inflow of nationalist men and material; but the revolution was not yet strangled. There were still great numbers of weapons within Algeria, and a vast majority of the Moslem population was sympathetic to the nationalist movement, if not working for it. In March, 1960, Dr. Frantz Fanon was appointed the revolution's permanent representative in Accra. From his new post, Fanon helped expand the flow of war materiel northward through the Sahara. He continued to plan for the beginning of an African army.

Under the provisions of the resolution passed at the 1960 Pan-African Conference at Addis Ababa, Nkrumah had opened two recruitment centers in Accra; he claimed to have five hundred volunteers ready to fight in Algeria. There were four other centers in Cairo with some three hundred volunteers. The Provisional Government of the Algerian Republic, in Tunis, was anxious for the arms from the south, cool toward the volunteers. Fanon, not recognizing this distinction, spent the summer of 1960 commuting between African capitals, pushing for new arms and troops for the third front. It was a hectic kind of diplomacy; he seemed to be living in airplanes and Land Rovers. . . . There was hope for increased aid from Liberia. After extensive conferences with party leaders in the capital, Monrovia, Fanon was informed that his scheduled flight to Conakry, Guinea, was filled. He would have to wait until the next day to get an Air France flight to the same city. His overnight expenses would be paid by the airline. That evening when a charming French airline hostess stopped at the hotel to tell him that the plane would be two hours late the next day, Fanon was suspicious. It was the kind of personal attention he had come to dread—especially after the 1959 incident in the Rome hospital. Revising plans, he and an F.L.N. colleague left the Liberian capital by jeep and entered Guinea through the dark forests surrounding the border town of N'Zérékoré.

Air France still had Fanon, under the pseudonym of "Doctor Omar," on its passenger list for the next day. French intelligence had arranged for the plane to change courses from Guinea to the city of Abidjan, in the Ivory Coast, a nation whose leaders still co-operated closely with the French government. Despite the fact that the final list didn't include "Omar," the aircraft was searched thoroughly at Abidjan before it was allowed to return to its normal flight plan. Fanon's diplomatic endeavors seemed to be hitting the French in a sensitive spot. American interests were strongly represented within Liberia, and it is conceivable that U.S. intelligence sources were working with the French to rid the continent of radical leadership. As proved by later events, the C.I.A. was well-informed as to Fanon's importance. . . .

In Guinea, Fanon put aside diplomatic tasks to join a unit of Algerians traveling through the new nation of Mali to find infiltration routes into the Sahara. He first set up discussions between the technicians of the unit and representatives of the Malian government in Bamako. Malian President, Mobido Keita, was already convinced of the necessity of aiding the nationalists. There were seven along with Fanon, two F.L.N. political commissars, two A.L.N. transportation and communications experts, two men from the army's sanitary corps, and a commando guide. They were headed northeast of Bamako, but the territory's main highway was closed due to flooding; they chose a road to the east that Fanon described as "a joke."* In the midst of dark forest areas they had to search out tracks of the last vehicle to have passed—perhaps six months earlier. Travel at night was almost impossible. Fanon loved it all.

He could never get over the feeling that as an intellectual and doctor he was apart from the core of the revolution; he wasn't fighting. At last, in 1960, he was on a military mission, back in the warfare. Active. He got along particularly well with the commando guide, Chawki, a major in the *Armée de Libération Nationale*. Small, lean, with hard eyes, Chawki had taken a degree in a Moslem university in Tunisia and come back to Algiers to study the

---

*From Fanon's diary in *Toward the African Revolution*. This, and the quotations that follow, are from pp. 177 ff.

French language and Western history. Unable to comprehend the contemptuous attitudes of the Europeans there, he traveled to Paris for a better environment in which to continue his reading. Eventually, he returned to help his father on a farm south of Oran. He joined the revolution in 1954, and was one of the A.L.N.'s more highly skilled desert commandos. Fanon and Chawki had long discussions on guerrilla tactics, arms, and the technology of modern warfare.

At Mopti, the Malian police refused to respect Fanon's letter from the Minister of the Interior; they wanted to check his identity. He refused. There was a stalemate until the doctor went into one of his practiced administrative furies. Fixing the head gendarme with his glaring blood-shot eyes, Fanon stated that they had already wasted too much time. The police would have to respect the letter or put them under arrest—they had no identity to show. He reminded them that the Minister of the Interior might be upset by any further delay, and refused to say a word more. The facial expressions seemed to speed the Algerians' clearance. The seven made their way eastward across the northern border of Mali, noting the position of French installations in the Algerian Sahara and planning for military staging areas for the African men and materiel that were, at least in Fanon's mind, soon to be ready for the war. Fanon jotted in a notebook:

> Everything seemed favorable, and the Malians were, for the most part, quite determined to help us in creating this third front. People used to speak admiringly of the odyssey of General Leclerc's march across the Sahara. The one that we are preparing, if the French government does not realize it in time, will make the Leclerc episode look, by comparison, like a Sunday-school picnic.

At Gao, where the huge Niger River flows northward toward the brittle desert, the local commandant of a Malian army post insisted on refitting Fanon's party with Arabic robes and better rifles. Afterward, the Algerians were able to shoot a bustard, a large, heavy, long-legged game bird of the region, as well as several deer. In camp that night, Fanon and his comrades ate well, talked, and relaxed—for one of the few times on the strenuous march.

Aside from the one police check, there was continued co-operation between Malians and Algerians that re-enforced Fanon's usual enthusiasm about the future of African solidarity. At Aguerhoc, the two commanding officers recognized the importance of Fanon's mission without anything being said. The doctor felt that "a whole immense collusion," latent until then, was coming into the open. They were far north of Gao now, in the dry, hilly country overlooking vast desert stretches, and they were talking strategy and terrain with the post commander of Tessalit, on the Algerian border itself. Soon the Algerians were off across sixty miles of dirt road, in Malian Land Rovers, to see the border itself, and to inspect the construction site of the new French airfield at Bouressa.

Fanon was intoxicated with the changing landscapes. The Niger at Gao, a gray road of water, under a gray sky; pink islands in the river appearing as part of the sky; yellow sand beaches on each side of the water inhabited by a people refusing to eat the Niger's plentiful fish; Gao itself, a city of cubist houses constructed out of mud in defiance of the gray sky threatening rain that never falls. Northward the sky clears; the temperature rises but the heat is less noticeable. The desert sand is alive with colors and shapes; the tints of rocks range from deep red to almost-blue. Small parts of the desert are suddenly inundated with rains; meadows and flowers appear. There is an abundance of game. And Fanon wrote:

> Even the sky up there is constantly changing. Some days ago we saw a sunset that turned the robe of heaven a bright violet. Today it is a very hard red that the eye encounters. Aguerhoc, Tessalit, Bouressa. At Tessalit we cross the French military camp. A French soldier bared to the waist gives us a friendly wave. His arms would drop off him if he could guess whom these Arab outfits conceal.

They were recording the strength and density of French positions all along the border, each of the team taking notes on his specialty. Fanon emphasized:

> We must work fast. Time presses. The enemy is still stubborn. In reality he does not believe in military defeat. But I have never felt it so possible, so within reach. We need only to march, and charge. It is not even a question of strategy. We have mobilized furious cohorts, loving our combat, eager to work. We have Africa with us. A continent is getting into motion and Europe is languorously asleep.

There was still the unbelievable energy, incredible optimism, the libido of revolution. Fanon was opening the southern front, stirring up the Saharan populations, carrying Algeria to the four corners of Africa, moving upward with Africa toward what he called

> African Algeria, toward the North, toward Algiers the continental city. What I should like: great lines, great navigation channels through the desert. Subdue the desert, deny it, assemble Africa, create the continent.

But he could come down to earth to work on more practical problems of warfare. He sketched out the alternatives for the third front: It would either continue to supply the nationalist forces already in existence within the Sahara, or else the nationalists could set up longer truck routes to move arms and materiel further north of the desert. Fanon advocated a third solution: set up new attack lines from the south with from 500 to 800 African militants joining the nationalist war effort (he does not make it clear whether they would be commanded by Algerians). The first wave of attack would serve to mobilize local desert populations against the French, to demonstrate the nationalists' strength. Fanon was very specific about how the commandos would carry on the war: They were to recruit new members within each tribal group they encountered in the desert, at the same time leaving behind three or four of the original volunteers. The new recruits would know the territory; be able to act as interpreters with northern tribesmen; those left behind would establish "listening posts," information-gathering centers. Fanon went into details of supply strategies and the weapons to be used. This section of his diary, which was part of a report given to the A.L.N. chiefs-of-staff, reveals the strangest blend of military realism and political optimism —the practicality of an army commando superimposed on integrationist reverie. That the Moslem nationalists would welcome the presence of black Africans is assumed as the strategy of the new campaign unfolds. . . .

Despite his perception of the strength of the counter-revolutionary elements in the newly independent nations, Fanon underplayed the factors that would disrupt supra-national radicalism: the egoism of certain national leaders, the profound influences of the differing colonial traditions, the hostility between Moslem and non-Moslem peoples in Africa, the truth that certain political figures whom he most admired had not secured their power bases at home. These were the forces amplifying the difficulty of opening a third front in Algeria and eventually eradicating the notion of an African legion.

IX
Unfinished Missions

The costs of the war had been very high; the Algerians, unlike the Vietnamese, were not prepared for an interminable struggle. In 1960, there was a small number of ideologues, like Fanon, in the ranks of the F.L.N. and A.L.N. who would settle for nothing less than complete victory—immediate independence from France and redistribution of wealth in an entirely socialized nation. Most nationalist leaders were pushing for an immediate peace that would concede to the Europeans extensive face-saving maneuvers of retreat, guarantees for the future safety of the settlers' interests, and treaties of economic co-operation preserving France's rights to exploit the territory's natural wealth. Whereas Fanon was one of the F.L.N.'s better-known hardliners, Ferhat Abbas, Premier of the Provisional Government of the Algerian Republic, cared most about ending the war through negotiations. A pharmacist from Sétif, Abbas had been active in Moslem nationalist movements during his student years; he had become a parliamentary deputy under the French administration of the territory. He had condemned nationalist violence as late as 1953, and only joined the F.L.N. in 1955 when reformist politics were no longer tolerated in North Africa. He was useful to the nationalists as a symbol of the widespread support for independence; he was made premier to show the F.L.N.'s willingness to negotiate. In his sixties, Abbas, who could hardly speak Arabic, talked only of the necessity of ending the fighting. One could by no means say that he was in charge of the nationalist movement—yet he represented a powerful tendency that was abhorrent to Fanon.

While the F.L.N.'s permanent representative in Ghana, Fanon was not as close to the power politics of Tunis; in Accra, he appeared restless; his English was far from perfect; and he wasn't involved in psychiatric work. He began to edit an *Information Bulletin* on the war, but the articles ended as extracts from lengthier accounts that he preferred to submit to *El Moudjahid*. There wasn't a large enough readership in Ghana to sustain Fanon's enthusiasm for the *Bulletin*. He began to work on a book that would be called *Algiers—The Cape,* an attempt to integrate the Algerian revolution into schemes for Pan-African unity while discussing violence in Third World revolution. The book never took shape, though; Fanon was spending more and more time traveling through French-speaking Africa propagandizing for the African Legion to fight in Algeria as a concrete step toward unity.

By May of 1960, Ghana and Egypt had some eight hundred volunteers ready for the war—at least on paper—but at this point the F.L.N. displayed a marked coolness toward the project. The nationalists announced that all they could accept from outside Algeria were the services of highly skilled technicians. The bloc supporting Abbas shared no part of Fanon's concern for Pan-African unity, nor were they interested in national liberation movements outside of the country.

In 1961 Fanon requested a new position as ambassador to Cuba. He didn't receive the post. Certain of his friends think that by then he was seeking roots—trying to return to Martinique, first through Africa, then Cuba. He knew that his island was not ready for revolution. Unable to immerse himself further in nationalist movements in French-speaking Africa, he wanted to begin to examine Cuba as a model for what might take place in Martinique. Fanon finally realized that the limits of his influence on the Algerian revolution were defined by his not being North African; but he had no great taste for searching out a new Third World base of operations. "What I fear most," he admitted at one point, "is becoming a professional revolutionary."*

In the summer of 1961, Algerian politics took a swing leftward. The first unsuccessful peace negotiations with the French had helped to cut the ground from under Ferhat Abbas. When Ben Youssef Benkhedda was elected the new Premier of the Provisional Government, Fanon felt more welcome in Tunis. The reconciliation was not thorough, however; the doctor could not find what he

*Simone de Beauvoir, *La Force des choses* (Paris: Gallimard, 1963), p. 622.

considered proper representation within the ruling councils of the F.L.N. He was still living with Karl Jaspers' idea that there is a solidarity among human beings that makes each equally responsible for every wrong and injustice in the world. Fanon could not understand a totally self-engrossed nationalist movement, one that ignored the plight of neighboring peoples suffering under the same kind of colonial repression. The Algerian revolution was part of the African revolution: A clear victory was not in sight—the fighting had to go on. Though a million Moslems were dead, compromises and adjustments with the French were out of the question. Fanon lectured that concessions from the colonialists were often the cloak for tighter rule. There could be no close co-operation between the Western exploiters and the Third World exploited. In 1961, the colonized were organizing the defeat of the colonizers; there was no need to accept compromises with Europe.

He was aware of the grave differences of opinion within the revolution; he knew that rival power cliques had not hesitated to order liquidations within the nationalist ranks. But he didn't think it would serve a useful purpose to publicize the political fratricides that would eventually split open the whole movement. The friends of Fanon now living outside of Algeria state that at the very least Fanon was troubled when he talked of the revolution after 1960. Fanon's colleagues still in Algeria claim that he was a realist, that he always knew of the rivalries and was prepared to adjust to quickly changing political circumstances. These people feel he could have continued to work and write through a more conservative phase of the revolution.

By 1960, the African revolution was losing momentum too. It became Fanon's unpleasant task to write the obituaries of the nationalist leaders who had appeared most capable of contributing to left-wing unity in the continent. First Lumumba: Fanon thought he might have headed a strong and independent state serving as a base to attack the Portuguese administration to the southwest, and the Rhodesian oppression southward. It was only late in his career that Lumumba swung leftward; in one of his earliest speeches he had praised the Belgian troops of Leopold II for saving his people from the slave trade of the Arabs to the north. Lumumba was an amazingly energetic civil servant who had entered nationalist politics with the sole desire of working out a peaceful evolution toward Congolese independence. Jail sentences increased his sense of *Realpolitik;* but he always thought in terms of compromises and negotiations. He had come to the United States for aid in keeping his new nation unified; this voyage, according to Fanon, spelled Lumumba's own doom. Too many in Washington and New York recognized the energy and increasing radicalism of the African leader; he had to be liquidated.* Fanon and Lumumba had no more than three brief meetings; they did not know each other well; Fanon was most impressed with his political potentialities, and with his last speeches showing a new awareness of the necessity of African unity against neoimperialism.

Lumumba, Fanon, and Félix Moumié, known as the "Ho Chi Minh of Cameroun," were all born in 1925 and died in the same twelve-month span. Moumié, from the northern, Moslem part of a colony mandated to the French after the First World War, was a medical doctor, and a much more doctrinaire leftist than Lumumba. Moumié, like Fa-

---

*"Lumumba's Death: Could We Do Otherwise?" *Toward the African Revolution*, pp. 191–197.

non, was small in stature and could not contain his own energy; after 1952 its principal outlet was the *Union des Populations Camerounaises,* the radical nationalist political party in violent opposition to the French-installed administration of Cameroun. In May, 1955, twenty-six persons were killed in nationalist riots throughout the country; the U.P.C. was banned; Moumié had to flee to the British section of the Cameroun, where he set up a government in exile. By 1960, Cameroun was independent of French rule, but its Socialist government was pro-French. Fanon met Moumié when he had become the Socialists' foremost critic; the two got along brilliantly. In the fall of 1960, during an air flight to Tripoli, Libya, Moumié explained to Fanon how the Camerounian President had just overplayed his hand by calling in French paratroopers to smash an anti-government uprising. Moumié was sure that the return of the European troops would kill the government itself; he predicted that his party could take power in a matter of months.

Shortly after this conversation Fanon was scheduled to meet Moumié in Rome; they were to fly back to Accra together. The U.P.C. leader never showed up; Fanon had no way of getting in touch with him. Moumié's father was terribly worried when Fanon returned to Ghana alone; then the message arrived that the son was hospitalized in Geneva.

Reporters pieced the story together slowly. Moumié had been taken to dinner by a Swiss journalist actually working for the French secret service. Becoming violently ill after eating, he recalled having had a Pernod *apéritif* with a strange flavor. By the time he was admitted to a hospital he had diagnosed his own illness as thallium poisoning. There were two agonizing weeks; then he died, a victim of rat poisoning. A warrant was issued for the arrest of the journalist; he had escaped to Switzerland. . . .

Moumié, Lumumba, and Fanon were three examples of a new kind of African nationalist: They had all passed through a bourgeois phase when they had been made aware of the dangers of the traditional restrictive nationalism—incompatible with any kind of true socialism. Moumié and Lumumba had the power to begin building a unified African socialism; but they had underestimated the ruthlessness of the enemy. The neocolonialist forces arranged for their liquidation. Fanon never had the same political power, but he too was being watched. His suspicious glances were in no sense paranoiac.

Late in 1960, after the strenuous trip across Mali investigating the possibilities of escalating the war in the south of Algeria, Fanon returned to Accra. Feeling awfully tired, he went for a physical checkup. A doctor noticed imbalances in blood samples and advised him to see a hematologist at his next stop, Tunis. His North African friends were disturbed by Fanon's appearance: he had lost ten pounds, and there was an unattractive puffiness around his eyes. He admitted, for the first time in his life, to periods of total exhaustion; he went for another examination to an F.L.N. health center. The doctors seemed embarrassed at the diagnosis; it was Fanon who eventually extracted from their circular conversations the word "leukemia."

The word didn't affect him the way they perhaps had anticipated. It was as if it didn't concern him—he had too many important projects to finish, no time for a terminal disease. He went back to work as if nothing were changed. Slowly the idea of death took hold: His family and colleagues were able to convince him to seek further medical treatment. But the facilities for more specialized analyses were monopolized by Russia and the West; Europe and the United States were out of the question; the F.L.N. had to arrange for Fanon to travel to Moscow. In a hospital just outside of the Russian capital, after extensive tests and consultations, doctors put Fanon on Myleran, today's standard medication for granulocytic leukemia. He was told to rest, and offered the facilities of a cancer ward in eastern Russia. Instead Fanon arranged to tour several of the larger psychiatric institutions in and around Moscow: He had always been interested in the research there in behavioristic therapy. He was terribly dismayed by the patients' living conditions in the hospitals: strait jackets, bars, prisonlike monotony; things as bad as at Blida when he first arrived. He was disappointed by the whole appearance of Russian therapy and research.

The Myleran was having some effect; he decided to go back to Tunis. In more than one medical conversation during his Russian stay, he had been told that the leading center for leukemia research was in the United States, at the National Institute of Health in Bethesda, Maryland. The Americans were beginning experiments with completely new treatments for the disease. Informally, Russian doctors urged Fanon to apply for admission there. By this time he recognized the larger similarities between Russian state capitalism and the American system; but he could not bring himself to contemplate traveling to Washington, D.C., the capital of what he called "the nation of lynchers."

Before the trip to Russia, Fanon had been working some twenty hours a day—exerting a final effort toward pushing the revolution leftward. Because it appeared as though the Algerians in Tunis were more and more concerned about the doling out of power in what they considered an already independent Algeria, Fanon turned toward the nationalist army as another source of revolutionary momentum. He had more faith in the men using the guns than those arranging the peace; warriors, hardened to violence, would be less tolerant of neocolonialist compromises. Fanon was impressed by the toughness and optimism of the general staff headquarters on the Tunisian border, where they kept a nonfunctioning Chinese artillery piece, a symbol of friendship from Mao Tse-tung (also the only material aid received from the Chinese). He made three excursions to the general staff encampment in order to lecture on the pitfalls of a successful struggle for national liberation. His greatest concern, by 1961, was that a Moslem bourgeoisie would replace the European settlers without any real restructuring of Algerian society. He had a naive belief that the army could supervise the growth of Third World socialism, remaining immune from the materialistic corruptions of the new bourgeoisie. There are tape recordings of Fanon's three talks to the general staff; but they remain securely guarded to this day—from the public and from the rank and file of the army—in the Algiers Political Commissariat, the military that was so little affected by the live presentation of the material in 1961.

In Accra, Fanon had begun a book defining the relationship of the Algerian revolution to the liberation of the rest of the continent. In March, 1961, knowing that he had cancer, he told his publisher, Maspero, that he had given up this idea to work on a more general study of Third World upheaval. By May, 1961, Fanon was working on the last chapter of *The Wretched of the Earth*. The book attests to a ten-week eruption of intellectual energies. He was worried, in May, that some of the descriptions were too vivid, too angry, the result of his feelings that so many of the liberation movements were being compromised or corrupted. During the summer, he rewrote the chapter "On National Culture"; he made several drafts of the conclusion.

Fanon had to fly to Rome to meet Jean-Paul Sartre, who had agreed to do the preface. Simone de Beauvoir, with Claude Lanzmann, editor of *Les Temps Modernes,* drove to the airport to meet the doctor.* He was already in the waiting room glancing about suspiciously. He kept getting up, then sitting down again; collecting his baggage, pacing around. There had already been two attempts on his life in Italy. De Beauvoir noticed the same kind of anger in his eyes that had hindered Giovanni Pirelli's biography of the man. In the car going to Sartre's hotel, Fanon talked feverishly about the nationalist war effort; he knew every detail of all the important military actions of the recent weeks.

The conversation continued over the lunch table at a small restaurant near the hotel. Fanon, in fact, kept Sartre talking—about the book, and Third World revolution in general—for twelve hours straight, through two meals and innumerable cups of coffee. At two in the morning Sartre excused himself; he was recovering from illness. Fanon complained to Lanzmann, "I hate people who hoard their resources," and in a light manner added, "I'd give twenty thousand francs a day to go on talking to Sartre." At one point, Simone de Beauvoir was encouraging him to get certain parts of his memoirs down on paper, or into a tape recorder. Fanon snarled back that he had a low regard for autobiographies. But he got along

*From de Beauvoir's memoirs *La Force des choses,* pp. 609, 610, and 619 ff.; and from an interview with Lanzmann.

very well with de Beauvoir, and quietly recognized the importance of her two volumes of memoirs already in print. It was as if he were testing her.

De Beauvoir, for her part, described the doctor as razor-sharp, intensely alive, endowed with a grim sense of humor, pointed in questions, brilliant in parody, and able to describe incidents that lived before the listeners' eyes.

Fanon attached great importance to the visit with Sartre because, first of all, he had always respected the man's philosophical tracts as well as his fiction. Sartre's writing on anti-Semitism had stirred Fanon considerably at the time that he was putting together *Black Skin, White Masks*. Secondly, Fanon knew that the world-wide reputation of the philosopher would aid in the dissemination of the message of his own new book. Sartre was at one with Fanon on two very basic concepts of modern history: that the real violence lies in the heart of Western civilization, and that the colonized are forced to choose violent struggle as the only recourse for genuine freedom.

Leukemia is a treacherous disease; there are periods of remission when the patient thinks he is improving; then, a more severe relapse. Fanon felt healthier in Italy; in Rome he mentioned being bothered by rheumatism; nobody talked of the cancer. In Tunis, he was weak again, and bleeding from the gums. If he bumped himself, atrocious bruises developed. Fanon admitted to his friend, Bertène Juminer:

> I know that I don't have more than three or four years left to live. I feel the necessity to hurry to say and to do the most possible. . . . But my Algerian brothers ask me to "spare" myself. Do the colonialists spare them? . . . You see, keeping up the pressure, I have

finished *The Wretched of the Earth*. I would have liked to
write more. . . .*

Then he temporarily lost his vision; he was thirty pounds
underweight; he collapsed in bed. He couldn't go over the
proofs for the book. Desperate for more time, Fanon applied to the United States Embassy in Tunis for permission to travel to the National Institute of Health outside
of Washington.

His superiors in the F.L.N., Minister of Information
M'Hammed Yazid and others, encouraged the voyage;
they had been dealing with the U.S. government for some
time in matters such as these, for the nationalists had
gained a kind of *de facto* recognition of their rule in Algeria
from Washington. It was the C.I.A., working within the
Foreign Service, that negotiated Fanon's transportation
to the United States (the F.L.N. cared nothing for the
trivial distinctions between the C.I.A. and the Foreign
Service).†

Ollie Iselin, member of the American diplomatic corps
in North Africa, interviewed Fanon in Tunis.‡ The black
doctor was a nice catch for the intelligence services (Iselin
had been in Air Force intelligence). Washington would be
able to fatten its dossiers on the leftist segment of the
F.L.N.; Fanon knew a lot about other African liberation
movements. His kind of thinking and activities were a
threat to Western interests in the Third World. The C.I.A.
wanted to ascertain his life expectancy. . . . Fanon knew all

---

*"Hommages à Frantz Fanon," *Présence Africaine*, 1ᵉʳ trimestre (1962),
p. 127.
†Joseph Alsop was the first to write about the C.I.A.'s role in bringing
Fanon to the U.S. (syndicated column in the *International Herald Tribune*,
February 22–23, 1969).
‡Iselin's name and biography appear in *Who's Who in C.I.A.* (Berlin:
Julius Madar, 1969).

this and detested the situation. A slight remission in the disease allowed him to postpone the decision through the summer. He was able to work on the page proofs of his new book that described the nation that had become the last resort of his life—

> Two centuries ago, a former European colony decided to catch up with Europe. It succeeded so well that the United States of America became a monster, in which the taints, the sicknesses and the inhumanity of Europe grew to appalling dimensions.*

In the fall, Fanon was unable to get out of bed at all; his vision was clear during shorter and shorter periods of the day. The choice seemed: to die peacefully in Tunis or swallow hatred to take a chance on new therapy in the United States. He might salvage several months, a year more of an active life. The Myleran treatment in Russia had given him the chance to finish *The Wretched of the Earth;* perhaps after hospitalization in Bethesda he might be able to go back to work on the project of the third front. The fall of 1961 was a crucial period in the nationalist struggle: The French had initiated new peace negotiations, but they were dragging on slowly. The A.L.N. had to keep up pressure on the French army; Fanon believed that the southern front might be a decisive factor in winning a favorable peace, one that would allow for socialism in Algeria and for the beginning of the unification of Africa.

In September, the ever-efficient U.S. Embassy in Tunis arranged for Fanon to fly to Washington through Rome, where he had a last appointment with Sartre. This time Sartre had to drive over to Fanon's hotel, where the latter lay flat on his bed completely drained from the trip. Sartre

* *The Wretched of the Earth,* p. 313.

tried to speak to him; Fanon had no strength to answer. His face was tense, though. He kept moving about on the bed as if to show disgust with his own physical condition. Sartre left, terribly saddened.

The C.I.A. placed Fanon in Washington's Dupont Plaza Hotel for eight days before allowing him to be admitted to the National Institute of Health. Since there were beds available in the Bethesda Hospital, one can only speculate on the reasons for the delay. Bureaucratic inefficiency? Or else those who had brought him there wanted a chance to grill the sick man without the interference of a hospital routine. The C.I.A. might have wanted its own physicians' reassurance that the black revolutionary had terminal cancer.

Fanon, at the time, was so weak that he had to hire his own private nurse to look after him at night. During the days, Iselin, who had followed him to Washington, would visit the hotel. A close friend of Fanon's, also visiting him daily, was present at a number of the sessions with Iselin. According to her, he never got a chance to ask questions: Fanon used what strength remained to lecture on Western decadence and the vitality of the Third World. Each of Iselin's specific inquiries would set the doctor off on just the kind of tirade that the investigator found least useful. Fanon's friend felt that whenever the patient's strength was up, he looked forward to Iselin's punctual visits: He was more confident about the future of the Third World when he could confront the counterrevolution incarnate.

Still, the delay at the hotel increased Fanon's suspicions and hostility toward Washington bureaucracy. Once in the National Institute of Health he refused, at first, to answer even medical questions with any kind of specific facts or accuracy. But his new doctor, J. David Heywood, a young hematologist from the Midwest, a Quaker and member of the American Friends Service Committee, was so different from the Americans who had brought him to the country that the two warmed to each other. They did not go into politics to any great depth, but Heywood was impressed by the patient's manner of discussing medicine and psychiatry.

In November, Fanon wrote to a friend in North Africa:

. . . if I'd left Tunis any later, I'd surely have been dead. No doctor can hide that from me. Where am I now? In the trying period after the large hemorrhages when the leukocytes increase their offensive; where, during a night and day surveillance, they inject me with the components of blood for which I have a terrible need, and where they give me huge transfusions to keep me in shape—that's to say, alive.

. . . what I want to say is that death is always close by, and what's important is not to know if you can avoid it, but to know that you have done the most possible to realize your ideas. What shocks me here in this bed, as I grow weaker, is not that I'm dying, but that I'm dying in Washington of leukemia considering that I could have died in battle with the enemy three months ago when I knew I had this disease. We are nothing on earth if we are not, first of all, slaves of a cause, the cause of the people, the cause of justice, the cause of liberty. I want you to know that even at this moment, when the doctors have given up hope, I still think . . . of the Algerian people, of the people of the Third World. And if I've held on this long, it's because of them. . . .*

*Text of letter from a new collection of Fanon's works, edited by C. Pirelli and published by Einaudi, Torino, in Fall, 1970.

Fanon sent another letter to his editor in Paris, Maspero, expressing the same disappointment at not having died in warfare.

There was a remission; Fanon felt amazingly stronger. At the end of November he was able to get out of bed. He was cheered by the arrival of the first copies of *The Wretched of the Earth;* it was enough for him to begin planning the next book. There were three possible subjects: a history of the Algerian *Armée de Libération Nationale* that would discuss the political possibilities of reinvigorating the revolution; a description of the extent and functioning of the F.L.N. organization within metropolitan France; or a very different kind of book, a psychological analysis of the death process itself that he would call *Le Leucémique et son double.* Fanon still had his wide range of interests from history to politics to psychiatry. At this point he was receiving a number of visitors: the Ambassador from Guinea; Roberto Holden, in Washington to raise funds for his Angolan liberation movement;* and Alioune Diop, editor of *Présence Africaine.*

Then a sudden deterioration; he had the symptoms of acute anemia. He went into comas, became delirious. At one point he thought the frequent blood transfusions were part of a plot to make him white; he moaned, "They put me in the washing machine again last night." In his weakened state he contracted double pneumonia; he died on December 6, 1961. The body was flown back to Tunis. Ollie Iselin, still on the job, went with the coffin.

Frantz Fanon lay in state in the Tunis airport *Salon d'honneur.* Numerous delegates from African nations ar-

---

*Pirelli and others had warned Fanon of Holden's possible ties with the C.I.A. Fanon either didn't believe them, or didn't care; he felt that Holden's party was more competent and radical than the other movements taking shape against the Portuguese.

rived to pay a final tribute. Krim Belkacem, Vice President of the Provisional Government of the Algerian Republic, said in a short speech, "Our sadness is even more intense because he leaves us at the moment when the cause for which he has sacrificed so much is close to victory." On December 12, twenty official cars trailed behind the ambulance removing the body out of the city, up into the mountains toward the border town of Ghardimaou, where the A.L.N. general staff had its headquarters.

Several F.L.N. officials, as well as Ollie Iselin—who was not adverse to collecting intelligence on general staff activities in this center of nationalist warfare—and a detachment of soldiers took the coffin fifteen minutes into Algeria in a deeply forested section under secure nationalist control. An A.L.N. commandant spoke over the grave, "We look forward to the day when you will finally be reburied deep in the heart of Algeria." *El Moudjahid*'s account of the ceremony added:

> In a valley, further to the north, there was the thunder of artillery. Two airplanes passed over at a very high altitude. The war continued—very near. At the same time, a calm enveloped the brothers who had come to fulfill the last wish of one of their own.

X
Certain Conclusions

Though Fanon lived amidst violence, and wrote about the prime necessity of political violence, bloodletting traumatized him. Fanon considered this a weakness on his part —one inherent in intellectuals. Although he had fought with exceptional courage in the Second World War, and had not the slightest fear of close contact with the enemy in Algeria, Fanon found that he could not really accept violence with the same equanimity with which he wrote about it. His sustained diatribes against intellectuals, in the end, might be considered severe self-criticism.* Some

*A point made by de Beauvoir, *op cit.*, p. 622.

would like to conclude that Fanon's revolutionary drive fed off self-hatred. But, really, this is too simple.

He wanted, first of all, to be a psychiatrist, but outside circumstances continually interfered. *Black Skin, White Masks* showed the first impact of French racism; there is hardly a mention of revolution in this work. He thought more of retreat—the Antilles, or Africa as a second choice. Algeria, as it turned out, was as far from the West as he could go and still continue practice and research in "communal therapy." He was by no means an apostle of violence when he left for North Africa in 1953; it was the violence of the French in Algeria that pushed him into this pattern of thought. There were open murders as well as a general, subtle repression. The lawyer Marcel Manville remembers a 1956 visit to Fanon in Blida during which the mayor of the town prided himself on the fact that his constituency had escaped terrorism and warfare during the previous years. The night when Manville was at the hospital Fanon received a telephone call from a friend asking him to go to an address outside of the densely populated part of town. The two drove there to see some twenty bodies of young Moslems from Blida executed by the settlers' militia on suspicion of aiding the F.L.N. Fanon's services as a doctor were useless; he explained to Manville, as they left the bodies, that this kind of carnage was less unusual in other parts of the territory.

There was irrational violence on both sides—Fanon himself recognized this in a letter published in 1959. But he denied that the revolution would go to the extremes of colonialism:

> We do not legitimize the reflex actions of our comrades. We understand them; but we neither excuse them nor deny their existence.

> Because we are building a new democratic Algeria, because we don't believe that we can elevate and liberate in one area and repress in another, we condemn with bitter hearts those brothers entering revolutionary action with almost psychotic brutality which was brought into being and sustained by a long [French] repression.*

The French helped him to understand other implications of violence: that in a colonial society all violence is turned inward; the natives kill each other rather than the settlers. Black Power theorists in the United States have found Fanon's writings particularly useful in helping to explain the high homicide and suicide rates in Harlem, Watts, and the other ghettos. Almost all of Fanon's strictures on colonialism are relevant to black society in the United States. He found that this internal violence decreases during a revolution when the energies of the colonized are directed toward political goals. Third World revolutions are the cathartic vengeance for decades of quieter colonial murders.

Fanon's critics sometimes compare him to Georges Sorel, who, in his later career, wrote as if violence itself, detached from political goals, were necessary and healthy. The comparison is inaccurate; Fanon was always acutely aware of the context of violence. Third World violence might at first be primitive, animal-like:

> I use the term animal, I speak in biological language, because the reactions [of the colonized] are only part of the mechanism of self-preservation.†

---

*In Charles-Henri Favrod, *Le F.L.N. et l'Algérie* (Paris: Plon, 1962), pp. 302 and 303.
†Fanon's speech to the Accra Pan-African Conference, April 7–10, 1960.

Third World nationalist parties have the primary task of channeling violence toward constructive political goals. These parties, originally set up by the educated elite, have had to expand into mass organizations in order to defeat the colonial interests ensconced in the underdeveloped areas for the last century. The mass parties, too, are created out of violence:

> . . . each individual forms a violent link in the great chain, a part of the great organism of violence which has surged upward in reaction to the settler violence. . . . The armed struggle mobilizes the people, that is to say, throws them in one way and in one direction.*

The new nations are built with a cement of blood and anger. When a large majority of the people have taken part in the struggle for national liberation, they will be less tolerant of individuals calling themselves *the* liberators. A widespread violent upheaval can lay the foundations for a widespread democratic rule.

A successful war of liberation is only the first step: Economic warfare has to be continued after the political peace. The West, according to Fanon, has plundered the Third World for a century; there must be retribution, or reparations. The newly independent nations, working together, can force such reparation payments by boycotting Western produce and Western capital, by playing off rivalries in the Cold War against each other. The economic warfare could turn out to be as trying as the military stage before it; but the stakes are just as great—the defeat of neocolonialism.

The Wretched of the Earth stands as a monument to Fanon's anxieties about successful liberation wars; the chapter on "The Pitfalls of National Conscience" might be

---

* *The Wretched of the Earth*, p. 93.

considered a Communist Manifesto for the Third World outlining the false paths away from the colonial epoch. Fanon's fury is directed against the new bourgeoisies that expect to rule after independence. They are a city-based caste sometimes including urban laborers who were comparatively well treated in the colonial epoch; more often, merchants scraping a share off neocolonialist ventures; and those infatuated by the narrowest kind of nationalism who would even seek aid from the former mother country to keep control of the poorer masses. The bourgeoisie that Fanon defines is an underdeveloped class—small businessmen, artisans, administrators, university personnel, army officers—lacking financiers with accumulated capital and short on highly trained technical personnel. They fit well into the shoes of the European settlers who have fled the territory, and are hostile to any kind of genuine socialism. This class has to oppose real national or Third World unity because the latter might stifle money-making and the accumulation of power in local strongholds. They have adopted, finally, the racist attitudes of their European predecessors. Fanon could describe the Moslem bourgeoisie in North Africa as boasting of its Mediterranean, European ties and fearful of Black Africa. In Ghana, he had to listen to the same class talking of "Arab vandals" who still kept women as slaves. Neither group of the same bourgeoisie wanted anything to do with the other; Fanon wrote that they

. . . have come to power in the name of a narrow nationalism and representing a race; they will prove themselves incapable of triumphantly putting into practice a program with even a minimum of humanist content in spite of fine-sounding declarations which are devoid of meaning since the speakers bandy about in irresponsible fashion phrases that come straight out of European treatises on morals and political philosophy.*

In the new states, as the lack of material progress becomes overwhelmingly evident, the bourgeoisie is forced to take cover behind a popular leader with a charismatic grip over the people, who urges them on to greater effort for a smaller reward. The huge size of the army and police force gives an indication of the real stagnation of the territory. The bourgeoisie allows the older national party to disintegrate; it was useful organizing mass participation in the struggle for independence but there is no need for this participation in the peace. The new parties become part of the apparatus for control of the people.

Fanon is at his best describing middle-class structure, present and future, within the Third World. As in Marx, though, his theories weaken when they broach specific methods of destroying the structure, doing away with the dictatorship of the middle class. Fanon is not so naive as to think that the new bourgeoisie will betray its calling—though he does launch an appeal for it to put at the disposal of the people the intellectual and technical capital acquired in the colonial period. Rather, he believes that the hope for a better future lies in the countryside; he begins to describe the possibilities for rebuilding more radical national parties based in rural areas. Such parties would have to remain apart from governments; they should become the means through which the people control the broad administrative policies. Decentralization can reinvigorate the countryside, "deconsecrate" the capital, hopelessly corrupted by European rule and thought. The Third World cities, overcrowded, decadent, capitalistic, nourish the bourgeoisie's distrust of the in-

* *Ibid.,* p. 163.

terior where the huge majority of the people live.

The duty of a revolutionary intellectual is to integrate himself into the interior, help with the political education of his people. Lectures to the masses are insufficient; what is needed is a dialectic. The peasantry is quite capable of constructive political activity if the proper questions are posed to it after explanations have been put forth:

> . . . political education means opening their minds, awakening them, and allowing the birth of their intelligence; as Césaire said, it is to "invent souls."*

Political education allows the masses to realize that, in the end, everything depends on their actions and decisions.

The Wretched of the Earth, as a plan for action against those who have expropriated the wars of national liberation, as a call for a second Third World revolt—against the cities and the corrupted militaries—has a disturbing lack of unity. In the midst of enumerating the perversions of decolonization, Fanon suddenly starts to describe the potentialities for renewing the revolution—without having given sufficient attention to the means of destroying the counterrevolutionary elements, the new bourgeoisies and their armies. In the whole book there are perhaps twenty pages devoted to the methods of combatting the corrupt but tremendously strong forces in control of the colonial areas today.

The plans for a rejuvenated Third World society depend on the intellectuals allied with the peasantry, a class that he has never examined with the care lavished on the new middle class. Fanon has given us a much more complete understanding of the meaning of true decolonization; his last work is most thorough in its compilation of

Ibid., p. 197.

the dangers threatening the decolonized; but there is not any thoroughgoing discussion of the rural antithesis to the urban degeneration produced by Western rule. One might return to *A Dying Colonialism* to learn of the rising expectations of the agricultural masses during the wars of liberation, but these seem to have evaporated with the evacuation of the colonial troops and declarations of independence. Fanon lacked time to put forth a detailed study of peasant class structure; it is in no way evident, from his writing, how the Third World bourgeoisie will manufacture its own doom. Today this class has a tighter control than it ever had in Fanon's time over the African and South American continents.

Then there is the crucial issue of industrialization: How is it to be carried out in the countryside? Urban concentrations of labor, material, and capital appear today as indispensable to the growth of industry; and without industry, the old colonies will always remain at the mercy of the colonizers.*

Certain Marxist scholars go much further in their criticism of Fanon's writing: too many generalizations in this last book, too little precision, theory not expanded to its logical conclusions.... But so often these scholars forget to feel the tone of Fanon's writing; forget that he was writing to *make* a revolution, not to dissect one.

Fanon is at his best in setting forth all of the problems of decolonization—in establishing the larger program for a cultural revolution. What is amazing is that a man, propelled by such fury, could see entire political panoramas with total clarity. The older systems of class analyses, ac-

---

*For a thorough and intelligent critique of Fanon's writing, see A. Norman Klein, "On Revolutionary Violence," *Studies on the Left*, Vol. VI, No. 3 (1966), pp. 62–82.

cording to Fanon, have to be revised; the great criterion must be to distinguish between the exploiters and the exploited. He described the Third World rural populations, and the urban lumpen-proletariat, as the exploited; Fanon's readers have gone much further—emphasizing the unity between the American blacks and the other *damnés de la terre*. Western student activists and intellectuals have, by choice, joined the exploited; and it is by them Fanon's writing is most understood and appreciated.

His continuing message was on the necessity

> to educate man to be *actional,* preserving in all his relations his respect for the basic values that constitute the human world. . . .*

Thinking, of course, is part of action. One has to have ideas upon which to act. The action in turn will lead to the revision of ideas. Theories must constantly change—in the light of activity—hence the contradictions in Fanon's own writings. Existentialism links Marxism and structuralism with reality. Political action is precipitated by the simple sentiment that the present social environment is not perfect. In 1955, Fanon wrote:

> To act is to have a system of values. To act is to propose a hierarchical order superior to that which exists.†

Action can end in "incoherent agitation if it does not serve to reconstruct the consciousness of an individual." Acting, too, must help restore communication between human beings, develop sensitivity, lead to revised social

*My own translation from *Peau noire, masques blancs,* p. 200.
†From Fanon's unedited notes at Blida, *c.* 1955, in Pirelli's collection of Fanon's works (Torino, Einaudi, 1970).

values. Despite a primary emphasis on motion and commitment, he reiterated:

> Action isn't an explosion. Action is a continual creation of a human order.*

For Fanon, existence precedes essence: That is to say, again, that theory is refined from experience. Fanon's psychiatric work has a structuralist tone that means that he is most interested in recreating man within the delicate balance of his environment—without condemning one society as inferior to another unless that society insists on dominating the other. The problem was that the white world ruled the black; the European settlers were crushing the Moslems; the French exploiting the Martinicans; Third World cities pulling the wealth from the countryside; the West building its prosperity off the labor and resources of the colonial areas. . . .

One might hesitate in attempting to evaluate Fanon's historical importance so soon after his death except that the doctor himself would have enjoyed this presumption. He was enamored of generalizing on the history of the future.

Though a great part of his life was devoted to psychiatry, Fanon will never be a major figure in the history of Western medicine. His reforms were very basic; his technical writings are interesting but not extensive or complete. So many of Fanon's articles in psychiatric reviews are expansions and generalizations from a single case history that one is reminded of Karl Jasper's contention:

> Comprehension in depth of a single instance will often enable us, phenomenologically, to apply this

* *Ibid.*

understanding in general to innumerable cases. . . .
What is important in phenomenology is less the study
of a large number of instances than the intuitive and
deep understanding of a few individual cases.*

Fanon was too rushed to make clear the exact links between the single case examined and the general psychiatric syndrome.

The same criticism does not hold for his survey of the
possibilities of creating day-care psychiatric centers that
could replace large, elaborate psychiatric institutions—a
way of decentralizing medicine along with politics. These
centers could be run by a minimum of doctors supervising well-trained nurses. Nurses, Fanon showed at Blida,
who would be capable of educating each other. With day-
care centers, therapy could be restored to its proper social context: the patients would retain contact with
families, work, and friends.

This survey was part of Fanon's major effort to improve
the medical care for the masses outside of Europe by
restructuring medical institutions. He was most interested in training a corps of teachers who could continue
to train others to give general care to a large number of
patients. The newly independent nations did not have the
time or money for medical schools and doctors; numbers
of well-educated nurses were immediately necessary.

In the West, quite obviously, Fanon's reputation rests
on his political writings—especially *The Wretched of the
Earth*, completed in three hectic spring months. The book
presents most clearly the notion that we are today sub-
merged in a surplus of wordage that has stifled radical
movement. Violence, Fanon showed, has to be part of any
genuine radical movement. *The Wretched of the Earth*

*My own translation from *Peau noire, masques blancs*, p. 156.

marks, within the black civil rights movement, the change from passive resistance to active defense; Fanon's writings are of central importance to the Black Panthers, representatives of the changed politics of black America.

The white American middle class, anxious to keep informed on that which threatens them, has taken to reading Fanon too. What better indication is there than *Time* magazine listing *The Wretched of the Earth* as one of the five most important books of the last decade? The sales figures for all of his books in the United States have blossomed over the half million mark. There will be, within the next two years, three other books on him in English following the first extensive study of his theory published in Germany.*

But Fanon's theory has to be restored to its proper context. *The Wretched of the Earth* was never intended as a detailed analysis of economic change; it is more clearly an *outil de combat,* part of the war against colonialism. Fanon wanted to redefine the concepts of industrialization and development; the Western ideal of automobile production was not always relevant to agricultural regions; had he lived longer, he could have extended and amended his thoughts on decentralization and rural revolution.

In the spring of 1961 he had one aim: to arouse, to excite, to anger, to activate those who were being exploited. He wanted to warn of the dangers of more subtle kinds of exploitation. *The Wretched of the Earth* was just a beginning; he had become a warrior only in 1956; a socialist perhaps as late as 1960. Detailed theoretical criticism of *The Wretched of the Earth,* though enjoyable, somehow misses the point. Fanon was a brilliantly skilled revolu-

---

*Renata Zahar, *Kolonialismus und ntfremdung. Zur politischen Theorie Frantz Fanons* (Frankfurt am Main: Europaïsche Verlagsanstalt, 1969).

tionary propagandist. This term "propagandist," in the United States, has a sour taste to it—perhaps because Americans have developed propaganda to a degree whereby they do not recognize the extent to which they use it. In the West we are brainwashed against the use of violence in politics which works to re-enforce institutionalized injustices. Fanon popularizes the effectiveness of violence—or even the threat of violence—among the peoples who are the victims of the propaganda of passivity. He is a war correspondent from the midst of the revolution whose passion and confidence can only draw others into the battle. The oppressed are given new life when a voice as strong as his announces (in the Preface to *A Dying Colonialism*):

> This is what we want and this is what we shall achieve. We do not believe that there exists anywhere a force capable of standing in our way.

Bibliography

The major part of this book was drawn from interviews. It would be unfair to list the persons with whom I spoke since this would unavoidably associate them with my own interpretations of the subject matter.

I found that published secondary sources were of very limited use.

Fanon's own writings, however, formed an essential part of the biography:

I. Books (American Editions)

F. Fanon, *A Dying Colonialism.* New York: Grove Press, 1968.

———, *Black Skin, White Masks.* New York: Grove Press, 1967.

———, *Toward the African Revolution.* New York: Grove Press, 1969. (Includes most of Fanon's articles in *El Moudjahid,* 1957–1962).

———, *The Wretched of the Earth.* New York: Grove Press, 1968.

II. Medical Articles

F. Fanon, "Réflexions sur la ethnopsychiatrie." *Conscience Maghrebine,* No. 3, (1955).

———, "Le Phénomène de l'agitation en milieu psychiatrique. Considérations générales—signification psychopathologique," *Maroc Medical* (January, 1957).

——— and C. Geronomi, "L'Hôpitalisation de jour en psychiatrie. Valeur et limites." *La Tunisie Médicale,* No. 10 (1959).

——— and ———, "Le T.A.T. chez la femme musulmane. Sociologie de la perception et de l'imagination." Congrès de médecins aliénistes et neurologues de France et des pays de langue française (Bordeaux, August 30-September 4, 1956).

——— and F. Sanchez, "Attitude de musulman maghrebin devant la folie." *Revue pratique de psychologie de la vie sociale et d'hygiene mentale,* No. 1 (1956).

——— and F. Tosquelles, "Sur quelques cas traités par la méthode de Bini." Congrès des médecins aliénistes et neurologues de France et des pays de langue française (Pau, July 20–26, 1953).

—— and ——, "Sur un essai de réadaptation chez une malade avec epilepsie morphéique et troubles de caractère grave." Congrès des médecins aliénistes et neurologues de France et des pays de langue française, (Pau, July 20–26, 1953).

—— and ——, "Indications de thérapeutique de Bini dans le cadre des therapeutiques institutionelles." Congrès des médecins aliénistes et neurologues de France et des pays de langue française (Pau, July 20–26, 1953).

—— and J. Azoulay, "La Socialthérapie dans un service d'hommes musulmans," *L'Information Psychiatrique,* No. 9 (1954).

——, J. Dequeker, R. Lacaton, M. Nucci, and F. Ramée, "Aspects actuels de l'assistance mentale en Algérie." *L'Information Psychiatrique* No. 1 (1955).

—— and L. Levy, "Premiers essais de Méprobamate injectable dans les états hypocondriaques." *La Tunisie Médicale,* No. 3 (1959).

—— and ——, "A propos d'un cas de spasm de torsion." *La Tunisie Médicale,* No. 9 (1958).

—— and M. Despinoy, "A propos de syndrome de Cotard avec balancement psychosomatique." *Les Annales Médico-Psychologiques,* No. 2 (June, 1953).

——, M. Despinoy, and W. Zenner, "Note sur les techniques de cures de sommeil avec conditionnement et controle electro-encéphalographique." Congrès des médecins aliénistes et neurologues de France et des pays de langue française (Pau, July 20–26, 1953).

—— and R. Lacaton, "Conduites d'aveu en Afrique du

Nord." Congrès de médecins aliénistes et neurologues de France et des pays de langue française (Nice, September 5–11, 1955).

III. Other Publications

F. Fanon, "L'Expérience vécu du noir." *L'Esprit* (May, 1951).

———, "Antillais et Africains." *L'Esprit* (February, 1955).

——— (editor), *Tam Tam* (February 21, 1948). (Only one issue published.)

——— (editor), *El Moudjahid* (1957–1962).

———, *Troubles menteaux et syndromes psychiatriques dans L'Hérédo-dégénération-spino-cérébelleuse. Un Cas de Maladie de Friedreich avec d'elire de possession.* Faculté de Médecine, Lyon, 1951–1952. (Doctoral thesis.)

Index